सीताराम

I0374127

Rama Shatanama Stotra

&

Rama Jayam - Likhita Japam Mala

:

Journal for Writing the Rama-Nama
100,000 Times alongside the Sacred Hindu Text
Rama Shatanama Stotra,
with English Translation & Transliteration

::

श्रीराम-शतनाम-स्तोत्रं

व

राम जयम - लिखित जपम

राम-नाम लेखन माला

(एक लाख राम-नाम लेखन हेतु)

Belongs to ______________________________

Published by: **Rama-Nama Journals**
(an Imprint of e1i1 Corporation)

Title: **Rama Shatanama Stotra & Rama Jayam - Likhita Japam Mala**
Sub-Title: **Journal for Writing the Rama-Nama 100,000 Times alongside the Sacred Hindu Text Rama Shatanama Stotra, with English Translation & Transliteration**

Author: **Sushma**

Parts of this book have been derived/inspired from our other publication:
"Rama Hymns" (Authored by Sushma)

Identifiers

ISBN: **978-1-945739-26-2** (Paperback)

—o—

www.**e1i1**.com -- www.**OnlyRama**.com
email: **e1i1***books***e1i1**@gmail.com

Our books can be bought online, or at Amazon, or any bookstore. If a book is not available at your neighborhood bookstore they will be happy to order it for you. (Certain Hardcover Editions may not be immediately available—we apologize)

Some of our Current/Forthcoming Books are listed below. Please note that this is a partial list and that we are continually adding new books.
Please visit www.**e1i1**.com / www.**onlyRama**.com for current offerings.

- **Tulsi Ramayana—The Hindu Bible:** Ramcharitmanas with English Translation & Transliteration
- **Tulsi-Ramayana Rama-Nama Mala (multiple volumes):** Legacy Journals for Writing the Rama Name alongside Tulsidas Ramcharitmanas—contains English Translation & Transliteration, Inspirational Quotes of Hindu saints, and space for you to jot down your spiritual sentiments on a daily basis. Once embellished with your Rama-Namas, these books become priceless treasures which you can present to your loved ones—a true gift of love, labor, caring, wishing, and above all—Devotion.
- **Ramcharitmanas:** Ramayana of Tulsidas with Transliteration (in English)
- **Ramayana, Large**: Tulsi Ramcharitmanas, Hindi only Edition, Large Font and Paper size
- **Ramayana, Medium**: Tulsi Ramcharitmanas, Hindi only Edition, Medium Font and Paper size
- **Ramayana, Small**: Tulsi Ramcharitmanas, Hindi only Edition, Small Font and Paper size
- **Sundarakanda:** The Fifth-Ascent of Tulsi Ramayana
- **RAMA GOD:** In the Beginning - Upanishad Vidya (Know Thyself)
- **Purling Shadows:** And A Dream Called Life - Upanishad Vidya (Know Thyself)
- **Fiery Circle:** Upanishad Vidya (Know Thyself)
- **Rama Hymns:** Hanuman-Chalisa, Rama-Raksha-Stotra, Bhushumdi-Ramayana, Nama-Ramayanam, Rama-Shata-Nama-Stotra, etc. with Transliteration & English Translation
- **Rama Jayam - Likhita Japam Mala alongside Sacred Hindu Texts (several):** Journals for Writing the Rama Name 100,000 Times alongside various Hindu Texts, with English Translation & Transliteration. Embellish these Books with your Rama-Namas and they become transformed into priceless treasures which you can later gift to your loved ones.
- **Rama Jayam - Likhita Japam Mala alongside Rama-Mantras (several):** Journals for Writing the Rama Name 100,000 Times alongside the Rama-Mantras from one lettered to thirty-two others. Embellish these with your Rama-Namas and they become transformed into priceless treasures.

-- On our website may be found links to renditions of Rama Hymns –
-- Rama Mantras/Hymns/Pictures are also available printed on Quality Shirts from Amazon. See our website for details --

rāma-nāma mahimā

In this modern era—which is awash with the six *Gunas* of Māyā: *Kāma* (Lust), *Krodha* (Anger), *Lobha* (Greed), *Moha* (Infatuation), *Mada* (Pride) & *Mātsarya* (Envy)—we find our minds sinking in worldliness. It seems that despite their best intent, no one can remain unsullied from the taints of Kali; this appears to be the fait-accompli of the *Kali-Yuga*—a very sad fate indeed. But despair not, because there is hope—we find ourselves assured.

The Japa of Rāma-Nāma (Rāma-Name) is the supreme path to salvation in this *Kali-Yuga*, assure our Scriptures; there is no Dharma higher than Nāma-Dharma in this Age of Kali—we are told. Sing the praises of the Lord and remain engaged in *Nāma-Smarana*—is the advice given to us by our saints. The chanting of Rāma-Nāma is The-One-Supreme-Path to escape the clutches of *Kali-Yuga*—declares Rāmachari*t*mānas—and in fact it **is the one and only Dharma which is easy and feasible in the present times.**

Many of the Hindu saints zealously assert: "In this Kali-Yuga, there is no other means, no other means, no other means of salvation—other than chanting the holy name Rāma, chanting the holy name Rāma, chanting the holy name Rāma."

Rāma-Japa—the constant repetition of the **Supreme-Mantra 'Rāma'**—is usually done mentally, or on a rosary; but there is one extremely efficacious method of this Japa: the *Likhita-Japa*, or the Written-Chant.

The practice of writing the Rāma Mantra over and over on paper is called the *Likhita-Japa*. This written form of Japa is a lasting record of your chant, remaining ever imbued with those holy vibrations, for all times, for the benefit of you and the future generations.

In India, as you may know, devotees of God have been chanting the name 'Rāma' and writing the Name 'Rāma'—pages upon pages of it, running into billions and billions, for ages. Hindu children are taught to write the Rāma-Nāma from their very childhood, and the writing competitions of the One *Lakh* Rāma–Nāma, brings up nostalgic memories for many Hindus.

The completed Rāma-Nāma books are variously utilized. Some devotees preserve them carefully for their holy association and divine energy, while others donate them to temples. The written Rāma-Nāma Books are used in the foundations of temples during construction; they add divine energy to the Temples—while in turn strengthening the foundations of the spiritual life of those who wrote the Rāma Name. Also some collected Rāma-Nāma books are placed in crypts to be used during *Yagna's* in Rāma Temples; and temples preserve these books for future. Devotees also place their own written Rāma-Nāma Books during the laying of foundation of their new homes, or in their *Pooja*-Room.

Of those of our Chakras (psychic centers), where our *Sanchit* (accumulated) Karmas are stored, Rāma is the *Beej Mantra*. The writing of Rāma-Nāma helps cleanse the Chakras, and our suppressed emotions, and the negative *Sanskaras* of the subconscious, and our remnant/unworked Karmas from past lives—which all get purged through the repetition of the Rāma-Nāma Mantra.

The chanting of Rāma-Nāma is a direct way to liberation. As per belief, devotees attempt to write down at least Eighty-Four Lakh (84,00,000) Rāma-Nāmas to get out of the birth-death cycle of Eighty-Four Lakh *Yonīs*, and thereby attain to salvation.

The *Likhita* Rāma-Nāma Japa is a powerful and transformative tool. As you write the Rāma-Nāma, all the senses become engaged in the service of Lord-God, and you find yourself simultaneously chanting and hearing and contemplating on the Lord—everything comes together naturally. This method clears away your thoughts and helps concentrate the entirety of your soul upon the Divine.

Any Japa is beneficial but somehow writing the Rāma-Nāma on paper brings up a great singularity of focus within the mind—and the peace of heart which ensues is something which is not so easily achieved with other forms of Japa. The written form of Rāma-Japa is somehow able to engage those parts of our body-mind continuum which other methods can not—and our meditative stance is able to achieve much deeper levels.

There is something special which will happen when you write the Rāma-Nāma—as you will discover. Peace and tranquility will surround you as you write the Supreme-Mantra: Rāma. The Rāma-Nāma will impart to you supreme strength, and great tolerance to withstand the vicissitudes of life. Bright unclouded wisdom will illumine your mind. You will find yourself in complete sense of surrender to your inner being. The resonance of God will resonate throughout your mind-body continuity. You will feel a flux of divine energy resonating within you. You will get great power and peace in your everyday life. The chanting of Rāma Mantra will protect your inner world as well as the outside.

Although the Rāma-Mantra is the gateway to higher consciousness and spiritual upliftment, but even at such junctures—when you find yourself in odd situations, where all the paths seem blocked—then just walking away from everything and simply writing the Rāma Nāma, will give you much needed clarity of thought—and a divine inspiration that will show the way out.

Thus, the Rāma Nāma is very transformative: with it you gain a balanced progress in your outside world and the inner. *Sant* Tulsidās says in *Rāmacharitmānas*: Place the Rāma-Nāma Jewel at the threshold, and there will be light both inside and out; i.e. a constant chant of the Rāma-Nāma from the mouth—the doorway to the body—will bring you external materialistic wellbeing, and also an inner spiritual wellness—both. Incredibly, with the Rāma-Nāma, you get to have the best of both the worlds.

According to the Vedas, just as the sun dispels the darkness, the chanting of Rāma-Nāma dispels all the evils and obstacles of life. The Rāma Nāma cures agony and showers the blessings of God; all righteous wishes get fulfilled; jealousy and pride disappear; life becomes imbued with satisfaction and peace; all of life's needs fall in place automatically—just like a miracle of nature guiding nature's forces. You may not always get what you want in the exact same form, but the Rāma-Nāma will purify things and bring to you the same needed happiness and bliss in a much more refined and lasting way. Your life will truly become filled with tranquility. Thus, with the Rāma-Nāma, an immense sense of spiritual wellbeing is experienced apart from gain of material happiness.

For *Likhita* Japa, you can write the Rāma-Nāma in any language of your choice—after all, Name is the connecting chord between the Divine and your inner self—but writing the Rāma-Nāma in its original Sanskrit form is simply superlative—most excellent, most effective. Sanskrit is *Deva-Bhāshā* (the language-of-gods). If you do not know how to write **राम** in Sanskrit it is quite easy. In the figure below, trace the contours 1-2 (which is the sound of underlined letters in the word '**ru**n'), 3-4 (the sound of underlined letter a in '**a**rk'), 5-6 & 7-8 (the underlined mu in '**mu**st') and lastly the line 9-10; and that's it. Note the similarity of English **R** , **M** to the Sanskrit **र** , **म** , (and English words used here like *Name*, *Saint*—similar to the Sanskrit *Nāma*, *Sant*.) All European languages have their roots in Sanskrit, the great grand mother tongue of most.

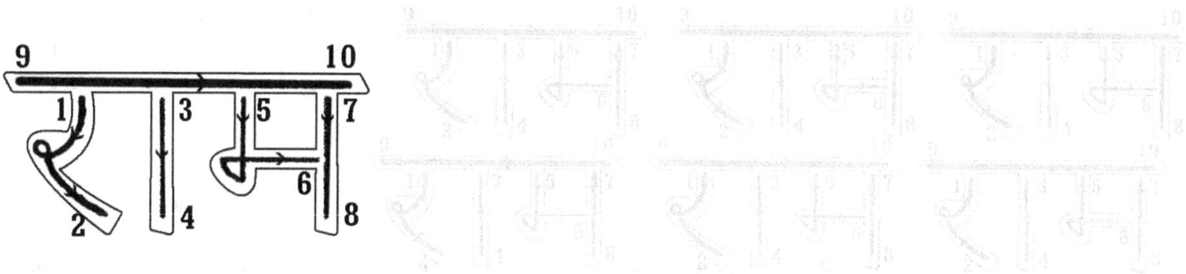

Write the Supreme-Mantra Rāma with reverence, every day, preferably at a set time, or as and when possible, in small measures, or copiously—howsoever your situation permits. There are no hard rules, do what feels good to your Soul. The important thing is to engage in the *Likhita*-Japa. When completed, you could keep the books in your Worship-Room, preserve them as treasures to pass on to future generations, donate them to Rāma Temples, or gift them to your loved ones—who will thereby inculcate crucial values from you, and learn the importance of the Rāma-Nāma, and get inspired with Hindu Values, especially so the younger ones.

While writing, focus your mind on the Rāma-Name and chant it within. Imagine Sītā-Rāma showering you with their bliss. Try to stay free of distractions, and with time you will find that your mind will take a natural meditative stance while engaged in the written Rāma-Nāma Japa.

You can choose any notebook or paper to write on, not necessarily this one. Traditionally people will write the Rāma Name in red ink on straight lines; but some devotees will also simultaneously make an interesting design—by changing the orientation of lines, or using different colors, utilizing an underlying outline to base their Japa upon. Do what comes naturally; no hard rules.

Find a set of pencils or pens which write and feel beautiful to you. If making an intricate pattern use pens that have finer points—but see that the ink does not bleed through to the other side.

Ideally, you will have a special set of pens kept purely for the Likhita Japa. This will make it easier for you to enter into the spirit of things. You will find that such implements—which you habitually use for holy tasks—build up energy and holy resonance.

A grid of 21 by 48 (1008 boxes) is provided for you as a guide—to be able to write a thousand Rāma Names per page. Some people will ignore the boxes and write in their own style, as and how their own inspiration leads them, creating their own design on the pages; and sometimes the design will preclude using all the boxes; but still, with 108 pages to write upon, and with space for 1008 names per page, you should be able to cross the 100,000 Rāma-Nāma objective of the book. The 100,000 target is merely suggestive—it assumes you write one Rāma-Nāma per box; obviously your mileage will vary, and you will get a figure more or less than 100,000, depending upon if you write smaller or larger. If need be, please utilize the empty spaces on the pages.

The pages contain the śrī-rāmāṣṭottara-śata-nāma-stotraṁ Text (108 Rama names in verse form) as font outlines. Before beginning your Likhita Japa for that page, if you can write within the stotraṁ outlines the Rāma-Nāmas—using color/size/slant which is different from the outside—then it will make those Verses stand out. Or if you cannot write so tiny, then simply color the verses using colored pencil or highlighter—that way the Text will pop out from amongst the waves of surrounding Rāma-Nāmas. We wish you Happy Rāma-Nāma Japa.

Once embellished with your Rāma-Nāmas, this śrī-rāmāṣṭottara-śata-nāma-stotraṁ book will become a priceless treasure which you can present to your loved ones—an unparalleled gift of love, labor, caring, wishing, and above all—Devotion.

—o——o——o——o——o——o——o——o——o——o——o—

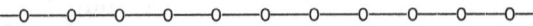

राम राम

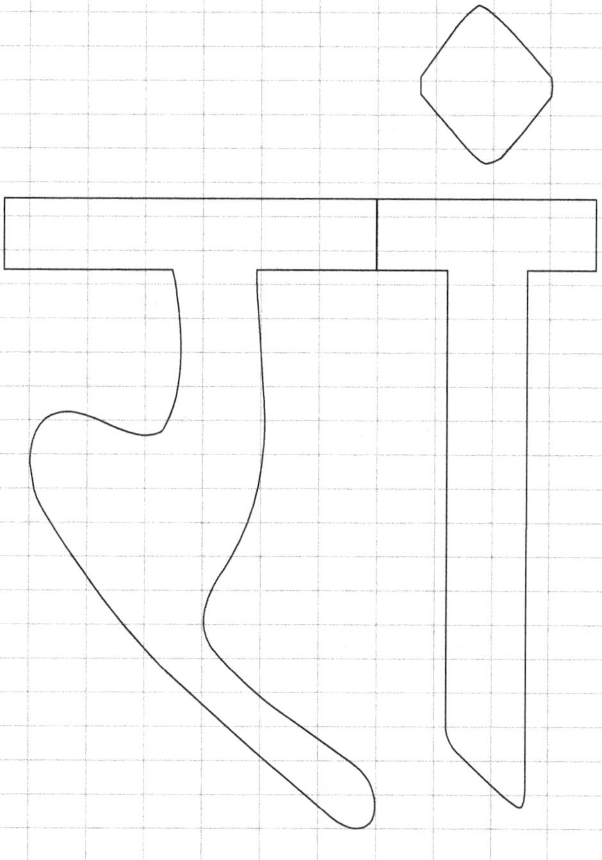

राम
राम
राम
राम
राम
राम
राम
राम
राम
राम
राम
राम
राम
राम
राम
राम
राम
राम
राम
राम
राम
राम
राम
राम
राम
राम
राम
राम
राम
राम
राम
राम
राम
राम
राम
राम
राम
राम
राम
राम
राम
राम
राम
राम
राम
राम
राम
राम
राम
राम
राम
राम
राम
राम

Today's Date : ____________

राम राम

राम राम

अथ
श्रीरामाष्टोत्तर
शतनामस्तोत्रं

॥ अथ श्रीरामाष्टोत्तरशतनामस्तोत्रं ॥

॥ atha śrī rāmāṣṭottara śata nāma stotraṁ ॥

________________: *Today's Date*

राम राम

राम
राम
राम
राम
राम
राम
राम
राम
राम
राम
राम
राम
राम
राम
राम
राम
राम
राम
राम
राम
राम
राम
राम
राम
राम
राम
राम
राम
राम
राम
राम
राम
राम
राम
राम
राम
राम
राम
राम
राम
राम
राग
राम
राम
राम
राम
राम
राम

atha śrī rāmāṣṭottara śatanāma stotraṁ

(Now commences śrī rāmāṣṭottara śata nāma stotraṁ)

Today's Date : ________________

राम राम

राम
राम
राम
राम
राम
राम
राम
राम
राम
राम
राम
राम
राम
राम
राम
राम
राम
राम
राम
राम
राम
राम
राम
राम
राम
राम
राम
राम
राम
राम
राम
राम
राम
राम
राम
राम
राम
राम
राम
राम
राम
राम
राम
राम
राम
राम
राम
राम

श्रीराघवं

śrī rāghavaṁ

(Obeisance to Shri Rāma - I)

________________ :Today's Date

राम राम

दशरथात्मजमप्रमेयं

daśarath
ātmajam
aprameyaṁ

राम राम

Today's Date : ____________________

राम राम

राम राम

सीतापतिं

sītā patiṁ

श्रीराघवं दशरथात्मजमप्रमेयं

śrī rāghavaṁ daśarath ātmajam aprameyaṁ

सीतापतिं रघुकुलान्वयरत्नदीपम् ।

sītā patiṁ raghu kul ānvaya ratna dīpam ,

______________ :Today's Date

राम राम

राम राम

रघुकुलान्वयरत्नदीपम्

raghu
kulānvaya
ratna dīpam

Bow I to Shrī-Rāma—son of Dasaratha, incomparable, the beloved consort of Sītā, the shining gem and leading light of the clan of Raghus—

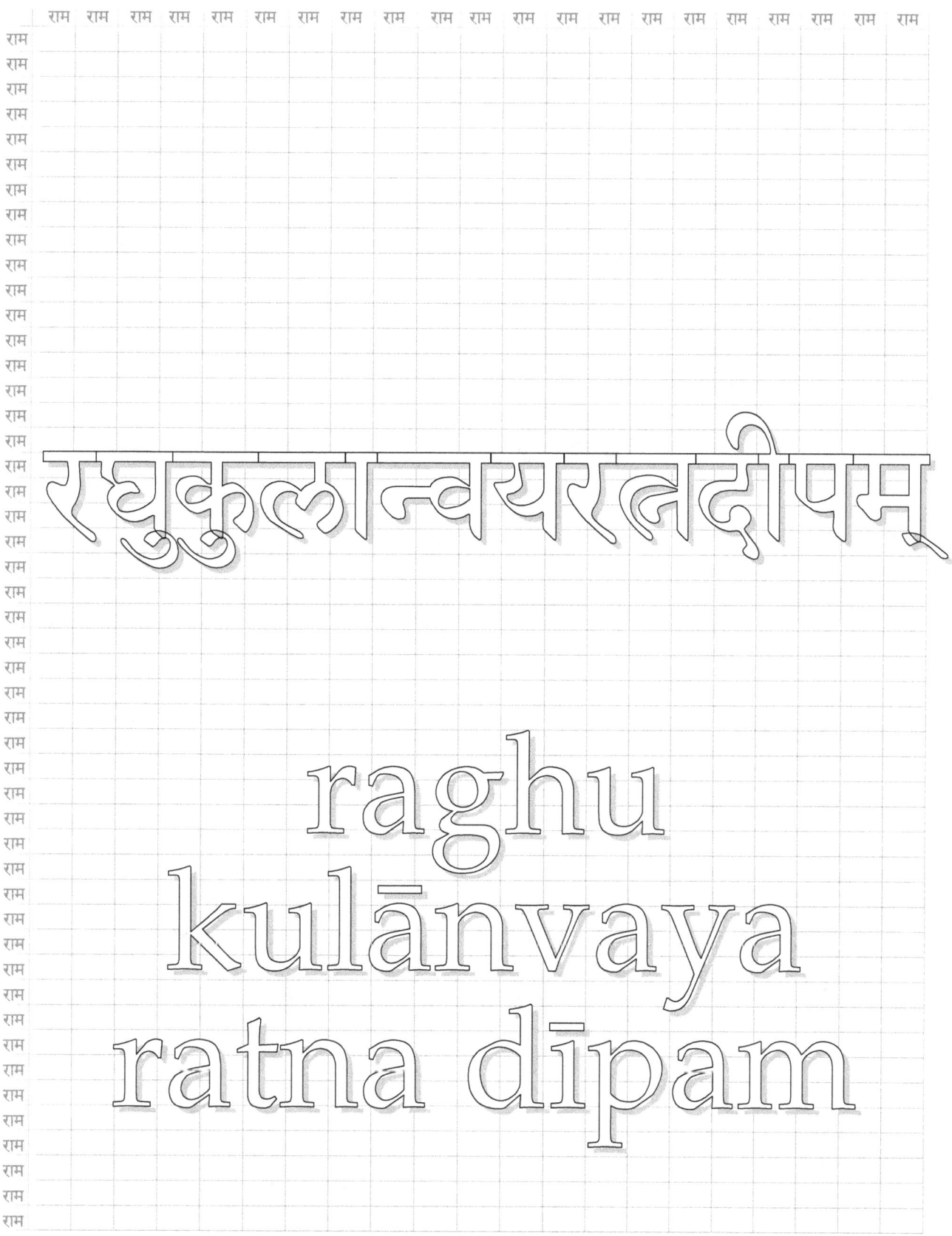

राम राम

राम
राम
राम
राम
राम
राम
राम
राम
राम
राम
राम
राम
राम
राम
राम
राम
राम
राम
राम
राम
राम
राम
राम
राम
राम
राम
राम
राम
राम
राम
राम
राम
राम
राम
राम
राम
राम
राम
राम
राम
राम
राम
राम
राम
राम
राम
राम
राम

आजानुबाहुम

ājānu bāhuma

______________ Today's Date

राम राम

राम राम

रविन्ददलायताक्षं

ravinda dalāyatākṣaṁ

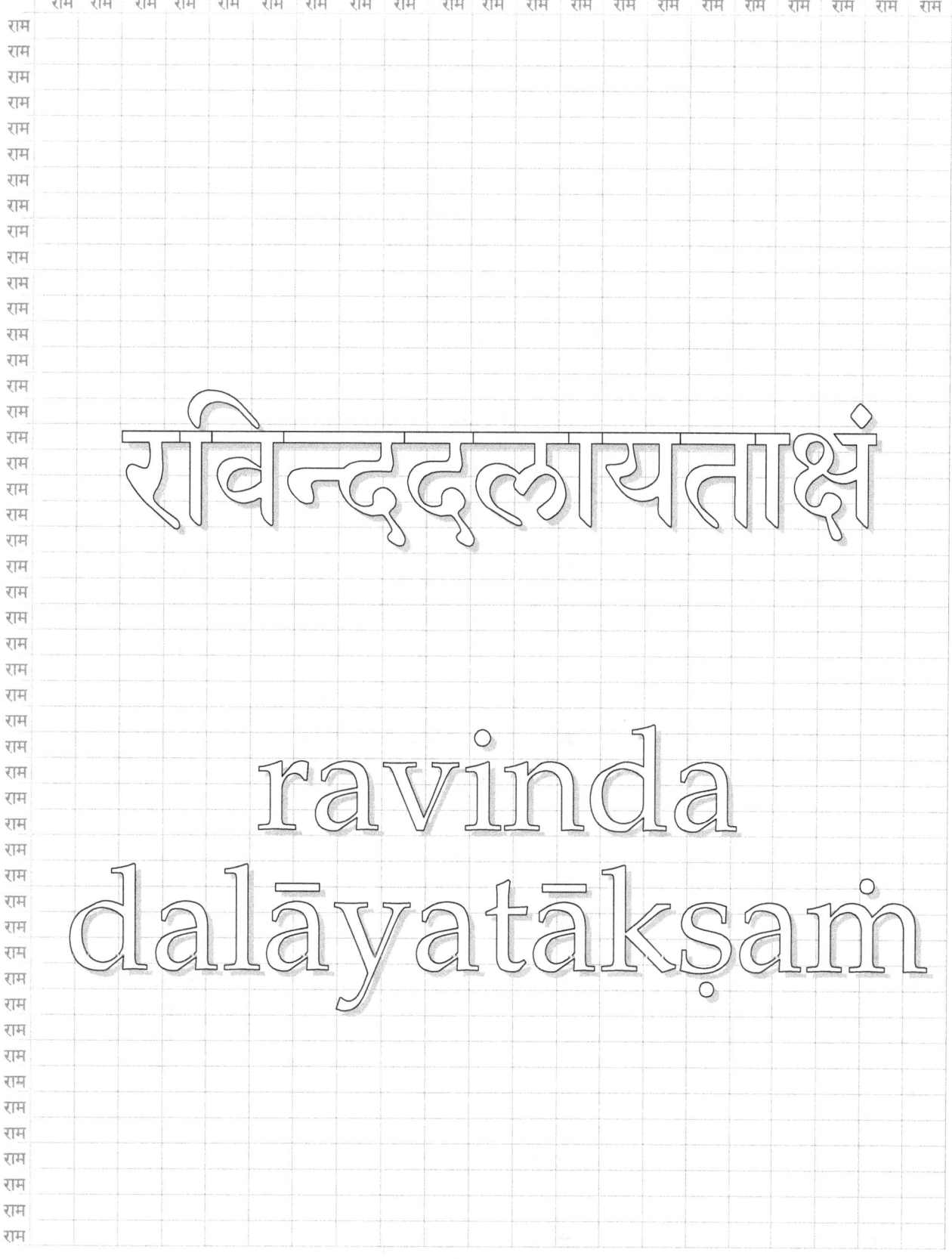

राम राम

राम राम

रामं

rāmaṁ

आजानुबाहुमरविन्ददलायताक्षं

ājānu bāhum aravinda dalāya tākṣaṁ

रामं निशाचरविनाशकरं नमामि ॥

rāmaṁ niśācara vināśa karaṁ namāmi .

__________ :Today's Date

राम राम

निशाचर विनाशकरं नमामि ॥

niśācara vināśakaraṁ namāmi .

—with long arms reaching upto His knees and eyes resembling petals of a lotus flower; unto Him Rāma, who is the annihilator of the night-wandering Rākshasas of the world, I offer salutations.

राम राम

राम राम

वैदेहीसहितं

सुरद्रुमतले

vaidehī sahitaṁ sura druma tale

(Obeisance to Shri Rāma - II)

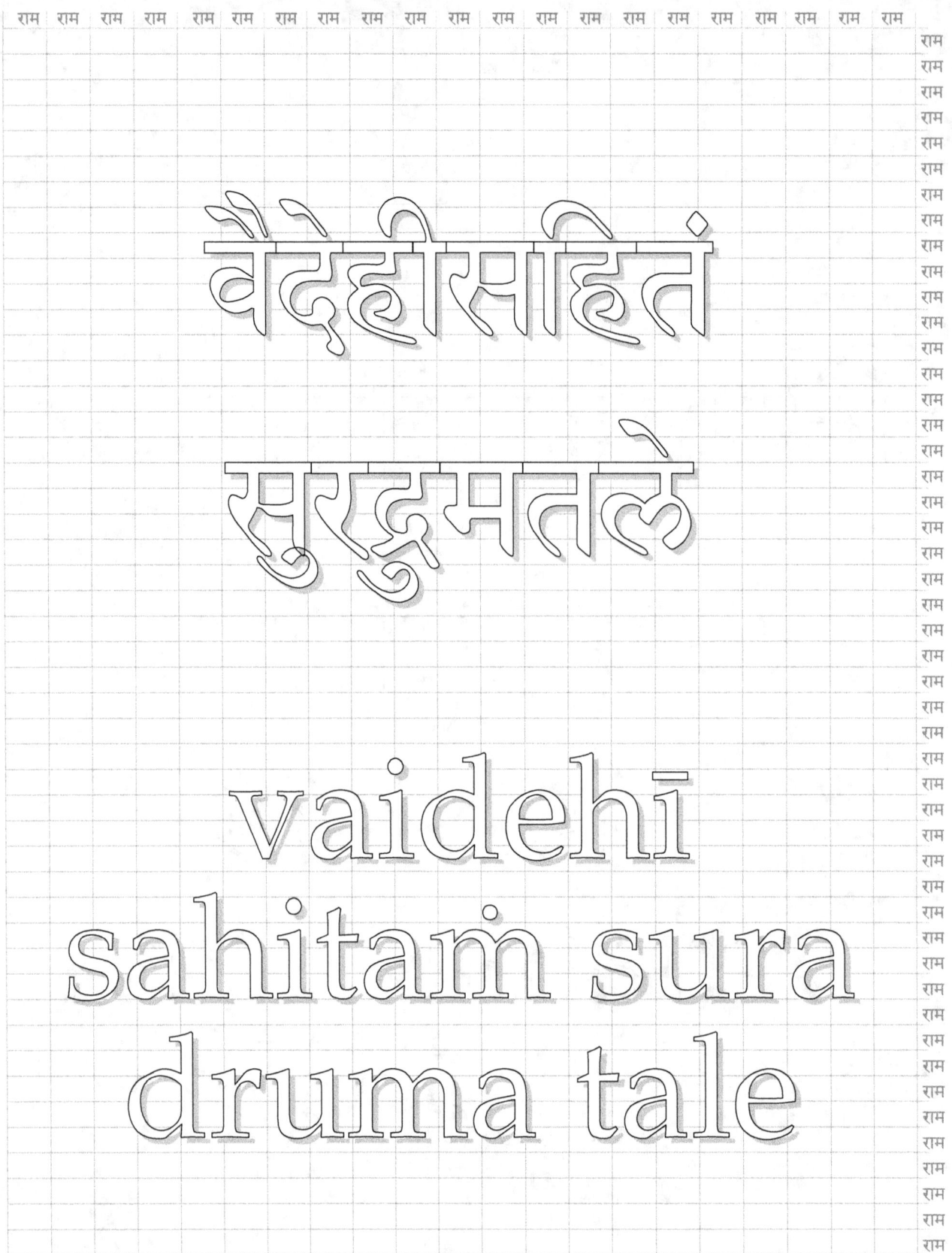

राम राम

राम राम

हैमे महामण्डपे

मध्ये

haime mahā

maṇḍape

madhye

राम राम

पुष्पकमासने

मणिमये

puṣpakam āsane maṇi maye

राम राम

वैदेहीसहितं सुरद्रुमतले हैमे महामण्डपे
vaidehī sahitaṁ sura druma tale haime mahā maṇḍape
मध्ये पुष्पकमासने मणिमये वीरासने सुस्थितम् ।
madhye puṣpakam āsane maṇi maye vīr āsane su sthitam ,

_________________ :Today's Date

राम राम

राम राम

वीरासने सुस्थितम्

vīrāsane susthitam

I bow to Lord Rāma who—along with His beloved consort Sītā, daughter of Videha—sits sporting the posture of the bravest hero, under the shade of Kalpavriksha (the Divine Wish-Tree) nestled in a grand gilded altar, set within the middle of the aerial Pushpaka Vimāna—upon a splendid throne constellated with gems.

Today's Date : ________________

राम राम

अग्रे वाचयाति

प्रभञ्जनसुते

agre vācayati prabhañjana sute

राम राम

________________:Today's Date

राम राम

राम राम

तत्त्वं मुनिभ्यः परं

tattvaṁ muni
bhyaḥ paraṁ

राम राम

राम राम

व्याख्यान्तं

भरतादिभिः परिवृतं

vyākhy āntaṁ bharatādibhiḥ parivṛtaṁ

अग्रे वाचयति प्रभञ्जनसुते तत्त्वं मुनिभ्यः परं

agre vāca yati pra bhañjana sute tattvaṁ muni bhyaḥ paraṁ

व्याख्यान्तं भरतादिभिः परिवृतं रामं भजे श्यामलम् ॥

vyākhy āntaṁ bharat ādibhiḥ pari vṛtaṁ rāmaṁ bhaje śyāmalam .

________________ :Today's Date

राम राम

राम राम

रामं भजे

श्यामलम् ॥

rāmaṁ bhaje

śyāmalam .

Encircled by brothers Bharatha and others, Rāma sits well settled—while in front abides the son of Prabhanjana (Hanumān) standing in veneration, enunciating the grand maxim: that the dark hued Lord Rāma is the Supreme Truth sung of and extolled by sages.

Today's Date : ________________

राम राम

राम
राम
राम
राम
राम
राम
राम
राम
राम
राम
राम
राम
राम
राम
राम
राम
राम
राम
राम
राम
राम
राम
राम
राम
राम
राम
राम
राम
राम
राम
राम
राम
राम
राम
राम
राम
राम
राम
राम
राम
राम
राम
राम
राम
राम
राम
राम
राम

श्रीरामो

śrīrāmo

(The Auspicious 108 Names of Shri Rama Begin from here)

________________ :Today's Date

राम राम

राम
राम
राम
राम
राम
राम
राम
राम
राम
राम
राम
राम
राम

रामभद्रश्च

राम
राम
राम
राम
राम
राम
राम
राम
राम
राम
राम
राम

rāmabhadra

śca

राम
राम
राम
राम
राम
राम
राम
राम
राम
राम
राम
राम
राम
राम
राम
राम
राम
राम
राम
राम
राम
राम
राम
राग
राम
राम
राम
राम
राम
राम

Today's Date : ____________________

राम राम

रामचन्द्रश्च

rāmacandra
śca

राम राम

_______________: Today's Date

राम राम

राम
राम
राम
राम
राम
राम
राम
राम
राम
राम
राम
राम
राम
राम
राम

शाश्वतः

राम
राम
राम
राम
राम
राम
राम
राम
राम
राम
राम
राम
राम
राम
राम
राम
राम

śāśvataḥ

राम
राम
राम
राम
राम
राम
राम
राम
राम
राम
राम
राम
राम
राम
राम
राम

राम राम

राजीवलोचनः

rājīva locanaḥ

राम
राम
राम
राम
राम
राम
राम
राम
राम
राम
राम
राम
राम
राम
राम
राम
राम
राम
राम
राम
राम
राम
राम
राम
राम
राम
राम
राम
राम
राम
राम
राम
राम
राम
राम
राम
राम
राम
राम
राम
राम
राम
राम
राम
राम
राम
राम
राम

राम राम

राम
राम
राम
राम
राम
राम
राम
राम
राम
राम
राम
राम
राम
राम
राम

श्रीमान्

राम
राम
राम
राम
राम
राम
राम
राम
राम
राम
राम
राम
राम

śrīmān

राम
राम
राम
राम
राम
राम
राम
राम
राम
राम
राम
राम
राम
राम
राम
राम
राम
राम
राम
राम

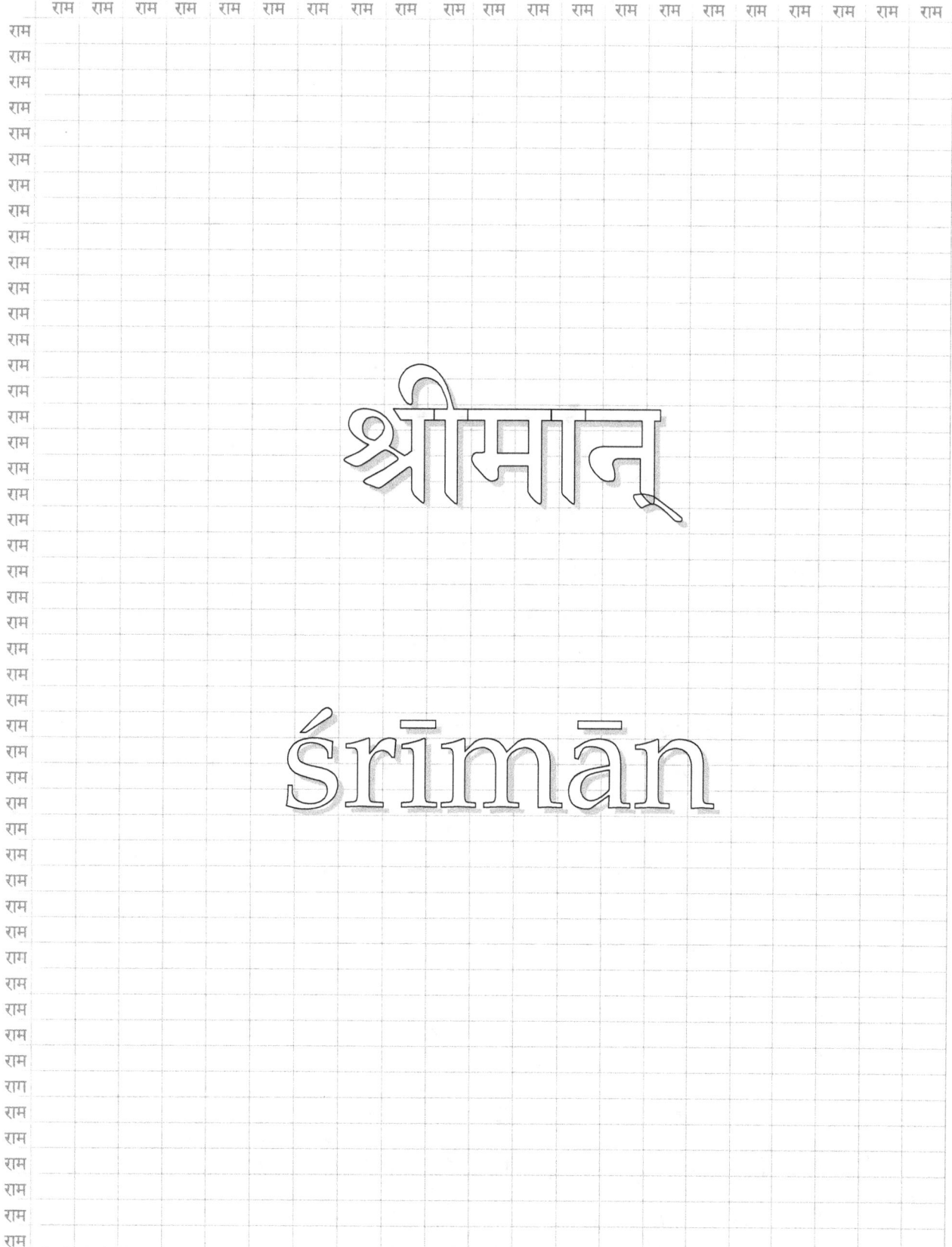

राम राम

राम
राम
राम
राम
राम
राम
राम
राम
राम
राम
राम
राम
राम
राम
राम
राम
राम
राम
राम
राम
राम
राम
राम
राम
राम
राम
राम
राम
राम
राम
राम
राम
राम
राम
राम
राम
राम
राम
राम
राम
राम
राम
राम
राम
राम
राम
राम
राम

राजेन्द्रो

rājendro

श्रीरामो रामभद्रश्च रामचन्द्रश्च शाश्वतः ।

śrīrāmo rāma bhadra śca rāma candra śca śāśvataḥ ,

राजीवलोचनः श्रीमान् राजेन्द्रो रघुपुङ्गवः ॥ १ ॥

rājīva locanaḥ śrīmān rājendro raghu puṅgavaḥ .1.

_______________:Today's Date

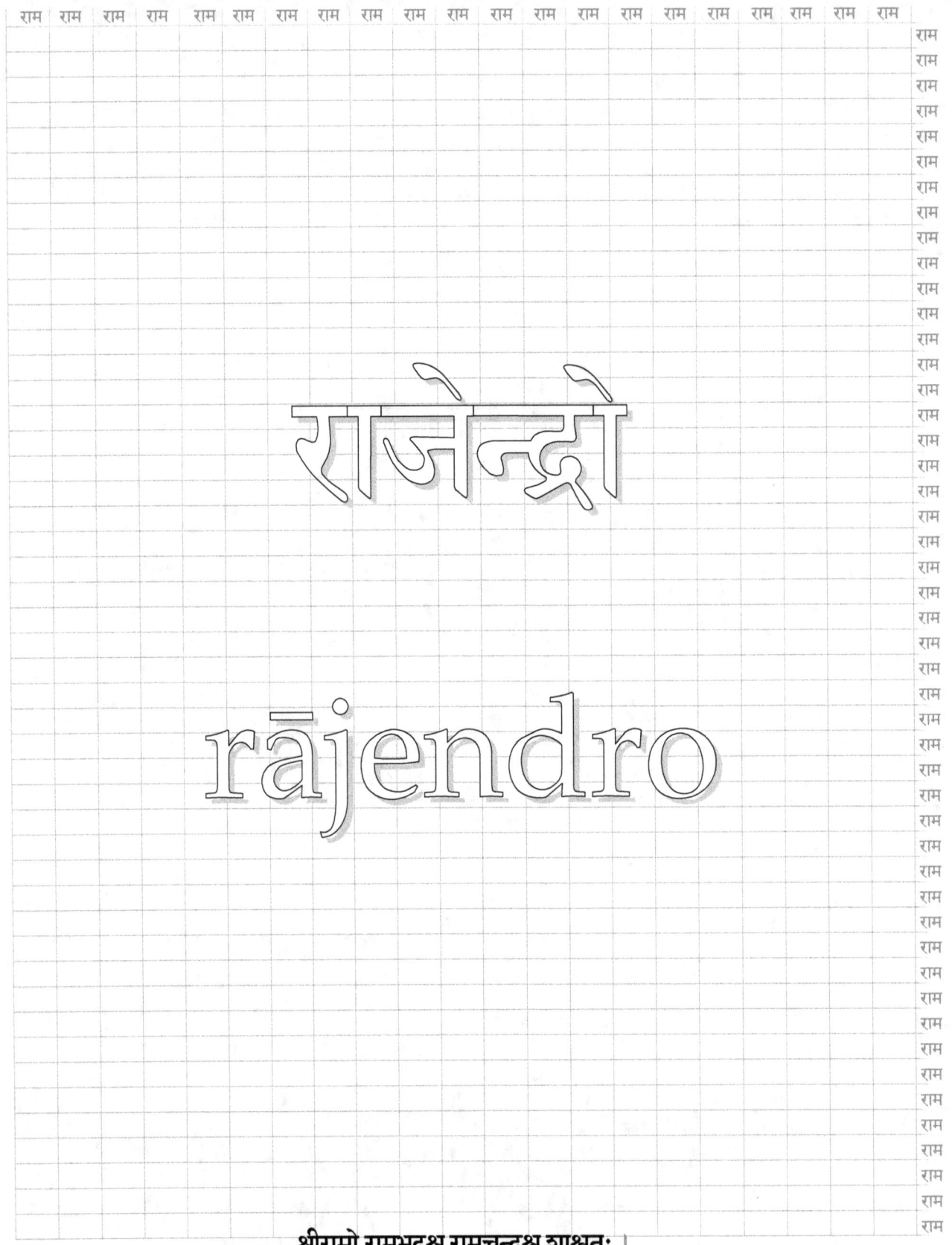

राम राम

राम राम

रघुपुङ्गवः

raghu puṅgavaḥ

Glory be to Shrī Rāma, Bestower of Felicity, the all-auspicious Lord, shining like the full-moon, the eternal Divine-Being of lotus-eyes, abode of Laxmi, King-of-Kings, the grandest Scion of the Dynasty of Raghus.

राम राम

जानकीवल्लभो

jānakī
vallabho

राम
राम
राम
राम
राम
राम
राम
राम
राम
राम
राम
राम
राम
राम
राम
राम
राम
राम
राम
राम
राम
राम
राम
राम
राम
राम
राम
राम
राम
राम
राम
राम
राम
राम
राम
राम
राम
राम
राम
राम
राम
राम
राम
राम
राम
राम
राम
राम

_______________ :Today's Date

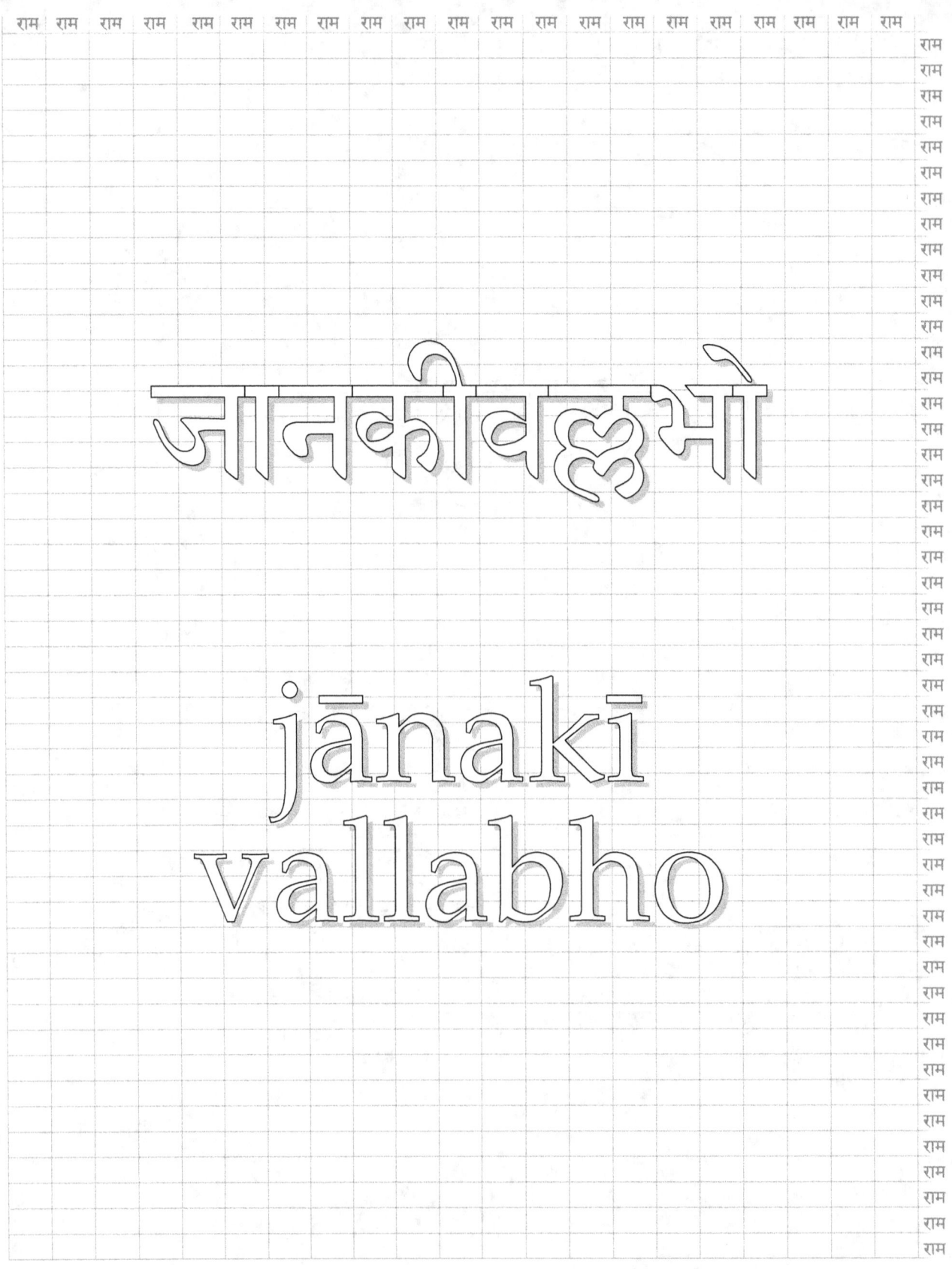

राम राम

राम
राम
राम
राम
राम
राम
राम
राम
राम
राम
राम
राम
राम
राम
राम
राम
राम
राम
राम
राम
राम
राम
राम
राम
राम
राम
राम
राम
राम
राम
राम
राम
राम
राम
राम
राम
राग
राम
राम
राम
राम
राम
राम
राम
राम
राम
राम
राम

जैत्रो

jaitro

राम राम

राम राम

जितामित्रो

jitā mitro

______________: Today's Date

राम राम

राम
राम
राम
राम
राम
राम
राम
राम
राम
राम
राम
राम
राम
राम

जनार्दनः

राम
राम
राम
राम
राम
राम
राम
राम
राम
राम
राम
राम
राम
राम
राम
राम
राम

janārdanaḥ

राम
राम
राम
राम
राम
राम
राम
राम
राम
राम
राम
राम
राम
राम
राम
राम
राम

राम राम

राम राम

विश्वामित्रप्रियो

दान्तः

viśvāmitra priyo dāntaḥ

जानकीवल्लभो जैत्रो जितामित्रो जनार्दनः ।
jānakī vallabho jaitro jitā mitro jan ārdanaḥ ,
विश्वामित्रप्रियो दान्तः शरणत्राणतत्परायः ॥ २ ॥
viśvā mitra priyo dāntaḥ śaraṇa trāṇa tatparāyḥ .2.

_______________:Today's Date

राम राम

राम राम

शरणत्राणतत्परायः

śaraṇa trāṇa tatparāyḥ

Glory be to the Beloved of Jānakī, the ever-victorious, vanquisher of foes, the redeemer of beings, dearest disciple of Vishwāmitra, self-disciplined, ever determined to protect those who take refuge in Him.

Today's Date : ____________________

राम राम

राम
राम
राम
राम
राम
राम
राम
राम
राम
राम
राम
राम
राम
राम
राम
राम
राम
राम
राम
राम
राम
राम
राम
राम
राम
राम
राम
राम
राम
राम
राम
राम
राम
राम
राम
राम
राम
राम
राम
राम
राम
राम
राम
राम
राम
राम
राम
राम
राम
राम

वालिप्रमथनो

vāli pramathano

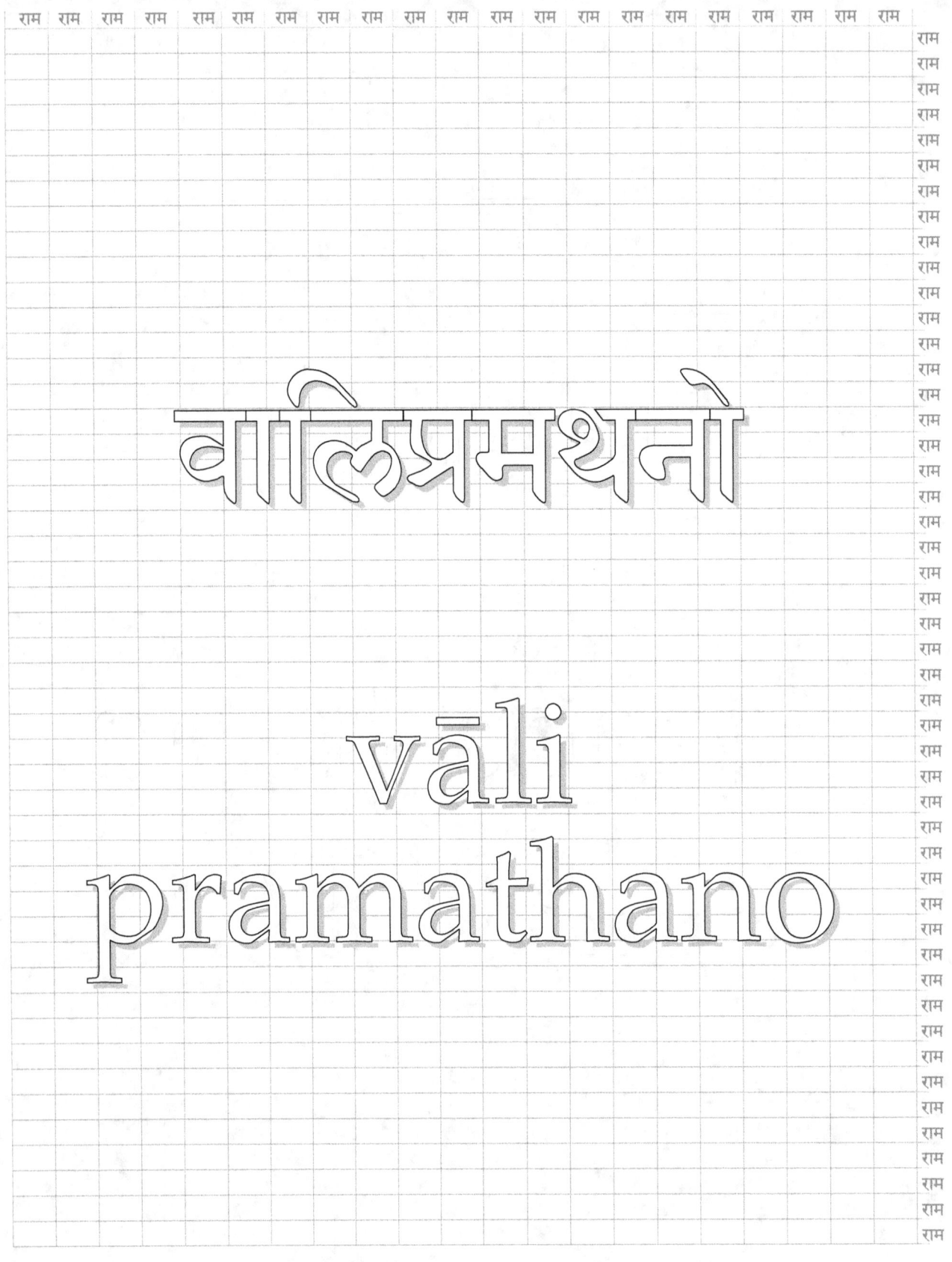

राम राम

राम
राम
राम
राम
राम
राम
राम
राम
राम
राम
राम
राम
राम
राम
राम
राम
राम
राम
राम
राम
राम
राम
राम
राम
राम
राम
राम
राम
राम
राम
राम
राम
राम
राम
राम
राम
राम
राम
राम
राम
राम
राम
राम
राम
राम
राम
राम
राम

वाग्मी

vāgmī

राम राम

राम
राम
राम
राम
राम
राम
राम
राम
राम
राम
राम
राम
राम
राम
राम
राम
राम
राम
राम
राम
राम
राम
राम
राम
राम
राम
राम
राम
राम
राम
राम
राम
राम
राम
राम
राम
राम
राम
राम
राम
राम
राम
राम
राम
राम
राम
राम
राम

सत्यवाक्

satyavāk

________________:Today's Date

राम राम

राम राम

सत्यविक्रमः

satya vikramaḥ

Today's Date : ________________

राम राम

राम राम

सत्यव्रतो

व्रतधरः

satya vrato vrata dharaḥ

वालिप्रमथनो वाग्मी सत्यवाक् सत्यविक्रमः ।

vāli pra mathano vāgmī satyavāk satya vikramaḥ ,

सत्यव्रतो व्रतधरः सदा हनुमदाश्रितः ॥ ३ ॥

satya vrato vrata dharaḥ sadā hanumad āśritaḥ .3.

__________________:Today's Date

राम राम

राम राम

सदा हनुमदाश्रितः

sadā hanumad āśritaḥ

Glory be to the Victor of Vāli, the Eloquent One, of Truthful speech, valiant in defending the Truth—of truthful Vows, practician of penance, the Lord-God ever served under the aegis of Shrī Hanumān.

Today's Date: ________________

राम राम

राम राम

कौसलेयः

खरध्वंसी

kausaleyaḥ khara dhvaṁsī

_______________:Today's Date

राम राम

राम राम

विराधवधपण्डितः

virādha vadha paṇḍitaḥ

Today's Date : ____________

राम राम

राम राम

विभीषणपरित्राता

vibhīṣaṇa paritrātā

कौसलेयः खरध्वंसी विराधवधपण्डितः ।

kausal eyaḥ khara dhvaṁsī virādha vadha paṇḍitaḥ ,

विभीषणपरित्राता हरकोदण्डखण्डनः ॥ ४ ॥

vibhīṣaṇa pari trātā hara kodaṇḍa khaṇḍanaḥ .4.

राम राम

राम
राम
राम
राम
राम
राम
राम
राम
राम
राम
राम
राम
राम
राम
राम
राम
राम
राम
राम
राम
राम
राम
राम
राम
राम
राम
राम
राम
राम
राम
राम
राम
राम
राम
राम
राम
राम
राम
राम
राम
राम
राम
राम
राम
राम
राम
राम
राम

हरकोदण्डखण्डनः

hara kodaṇḍa khaṇḍanaḥ

Glory be to Kausalyā's son, Destroyer of the demon Khara, skillful in subjugating the monster Virādha, the Protector of Vibhishan—the One who broke the mighty Bow of Shiva.

Today's Date : ___________

राम राम

सप्ततालप्रभेत्ता च

saptatāla prabhettā ca

राम राम

राम राम

दशग्रीवशिरोहरः

daśagrīva śiro haraḥ

राम राम

राम राम

जामदग्न्य

महादर्पदलन

jāmadagnya mahādarpa dalana

सप्ततालप्रभेत्ता च दशग्रीवशिरोहरः ।

sapta tāla pra bhettā ca daśa grīva śiro haraḥ ,

जामदग्न्यमहादर्पदलनस्ताटकान्तकः ॥ ५ ॥

jāma dagnya mahā darpa dalanas tāṭak āntakaḥ .5.

_______________ :Today's Date

राम राम

राम राम

ताटकान्तकः

tāṭakāntakaḥ

Glory be to the Valorous Rāma who pierced the seven Tāla Trees with a single arrow, who cut off the ten-heads of Rāvan, who shattered the inordinate arrogance of Jamadagni's son, and who slew Tāṭakā the terrible demon.

Today's Date : ____________________

राम राम

राम
राम
राम
राम
राम
राम
राम
राम
राम
राम
राम
राम
राम
राम
राम
राम
राम
राम
राम
राम
राम
राम
राम
राम
राम
राम
राम
राम
राम
राम
राम
राम
राम
राम
राम
राम
राम
राम
राम
राम
राम
राम
राम

वेदान्तसारो

वेदात्मा

vedāntasāro

vedātmā

________________ :Today's Date

भवरोगस्य भेषजम्

bhavarogasya bheṣajam

Today's Date : ____________________

राम राम

दूषणात्रिशिरो हन्ता

dūṣaṇa triśiro hantā

राम राम

वेदान्तसारो वेदात्मा भवरोगस्य भेषजम् ।

vedānta sāro ved ātmā bhava rogasya bheṣajam ,

दूषणत्रिशिरो हन्ता त्रिमूर्तिस्त्रिगुणात्मकः ॥ ६ ॥

dūṣaṇa tri śiro hantā tri mūrtis triguṇ ātmakaḥ .6.

________________:Today's Date

राम राम

त्रिमूर्ति त्रिगुणात्मकः

trimūrti trigun ātmakaḥ

Glory be to Rāma, the Essence of Vedānta, the Personification of the Vedas, Reliever of all earthly ailments, the slayer of monsters Dūṣaṇa & Triśira, the Lord-God manifest as the Trinity of Brahmmā, Vishnu, Mahesh—and from whom emanate the three gunas of Māyā.

Today's Date : ________________

राम राम

त्रिविक्रम

त्रिलोकात्मा

trivikrama
trilokātmā

राम
राम
राम
राम
राम
राम
राम
राम
राम
राम
राम
राम
राम
राम
राम
राम
राम
राम
राम
राम
राम
राम
राम
राम
राम
राम
राम
राम
राम
राम
राम
राम
राम
राम
राम
राम
राम
राम
राम
राम
राम
राम
राम
राम
राम
राम
राम
राम

____________________:Today's Date

राम राम

पुण्यचारित्रकीर्तनः

puṇya cāritra kīrtanaḥ

Today's Date : ____________________

राम राम

त्रिलोकरक्षको धन्वी

trilokarakṣako dhanvī

राम राम

त्रिविक्रमस्त्रिलोकात्मा पुण्यचारित्रकीर्तनः ।
tri vikramas trilok ātmā puṇya cāritra kīrtanaḥ ,
त्रिलोकरक्षको धन्वी दण्डकारण्यपावनः ॥ ७ ॥
tri loka rakṣako dhanvī daṇḍak āraṇya pāvanaḥ .7.

__________________ :Today's Date

राम राम

राम राम

दण्डकारण्यपावनः

daṇḍakāraṇya pāvanaḥ

Glory be to the Lord who spanned the Three-Regions of the Universe with His feet, the Lord-God pervaded throughout earth, hell and heaven, whose hallowed deeds are sung through Hymns, who's the Protector of the Three-Worlds, the Wielder of the Bow, and who sanctifed the Dandaka forest by dwelling there.

Today's Date : ________________

राम राम

राम
राम
राम
राम
राम
राम
राम
राम
राम
राम
राम
राम
राम
राम
राम

अहल्याशापशमनः

राम
राम
राम
राम
राम
राम
राम
राम
राम
राम
राम

ahalyā śāpa śamanaḥ

राम
राम
राम
राम
राम
राम
राम
राम
राम
राम
राम
राम
राम
राम
राम
राम
राम
राम
राम
राम
राम
राम

______________:Today's Date

राम राम

राम राम

पितृभक्तो वरप्रदः

pitṛ bhakto vara pradaḥ

राम राम

राम राम

जितेन्द्रियो

जितक्रोधो

jitendriyo
jita krodho

अहल्याशापशमनः पितृभक्तो वरप्रदः ।

ahalyā śāpa śamanaḥ pitṛ bhakto vara pradaḥ ,

जितेन्द्रियो जितक्रोधो जितामित्रो जगद्गुरुः ॥ ८ ॥

jit endriyo jita krodho jitā mitro jagad guruḥ .8.

______________:Today's Date

राम राम

राम
राम
राम
राम
राम
राम
राम
राम
राम
राम
राम
राम
राम
राम
राम
राम
राम
राम
राम
राम
राम
राम
राम
राम
राम
राम
राम
राम
राम
राम
राम
राम
राम
राम
राम
राम
राम
राम
राम
राम
राम
राम
राम
राम
राम
राम
राम
राम

जितामित्रो जगद्गुरुः

jitā mitro jagad guruḥ

Glory be to Shrī-Rāma, the Remover of Ahalyā's curse, ever devoted to His father Dashrath, the Conferrer of boons, Conqueror of sense-organs, the Victor over anger, who wins over friends—and who is the supreme Guru of the whole world.

Today's Date : ________________

राम राम

राम
राम
राम
राम
राम
राम
राम
राम
राम
राम
राम
राम
राम
राम
राम
राम
राम
राम
राम
राम
राम
राम
राम
राम
राम
राम
राम
राम
राम
राम
राम
राम
राम
राम
राम
राम
राम
राम
राम
राम
राम
राम
राम
राम
राम
राम
राम
राम

ऋक्षवानरसंघाती

ṛkṣa vānara saṁghātī

________________:Today's Date

राम राम

राम राम

चित्रकूटसमाश्रयः

citrakūṭa samāśrayaḥ

राम राम

राम राम

जयन्तत्राणवरदः

jayanta trāṇa varadaḥ

ऋक्षवानरसंघाती चित्रकूटसमाश्रयः ।

ṛkṣa vānara saṁghātī citra kūṭa sam āśrayaḥ ,

जयन्तत्राणवरदः सुमित्रापुत्रसेवितः ॥ ९ ॥

jayanta trāṇa varadaḥ sumitrā putra sevitaḥ .9.

_______________ :Today's Date

राम राम

राम राम

सुमित्रापुत्रसेवितः

sumitrā putra sevitaḥ

Glory be to Shrī-Rāma—the Lord who presided over the hosts of bears and monkeys, who dwelt at the Chitrakūta Hill, who saved Jayanta—the Lord-God ever served by Sumitrā's son Lakshman.

राम राम

राम राम

सर्वदेवादिदेवश्च

sarva devādi deva śca

__________________:Today's Date

राम राम

मृतवानरजीवनः

mṛta vānara jīvanaḥ

Today's Date : ____________

राम राम

राम राम

मायामारीचहन्ता च

māyā mārica hantā ca

सर्वदेवादिदेवश्च मृतवानरजीवनः ।

sarva dev ādi deva śca mṛta vānara jīvanaḥ ,

मायामारीचहन्ता च महादेवो महाभुजः ॥ १० ॥

māyā mārīca hantā ca mahā devo mahā bhujaḥ .10.

_______________:Today's Date

राम राम

राम राम

महादेवो

महाभुजः

mahā devo mahā bhujaḥ

Glory be to the God of gods Rāma—the Lord who revived the dead monkeys, the slayer of Maricha, the illusion practicing demon—the Greatest-God of mighty arms.

Today's Date : ________________

राम राम

राम राम

सर्वदेवस्तुतः

सौम्यो

sarva deva stutaḥ saumyo

_______________ :Today's Date

ब्रह्मण्यो

मुनिसंस्तुतः

brahmaṇyo

muni

saṁstutaḥ

राम राम

महायोगी

महोदारः

mahā yogī maho dāraḥ

सर्वदेवस्तुतः सौम्यो ब्रह्मण्यो मुनिसंस्तुतः ।
sarva deva stutaḥ saumyo brahm aṇyo muni saṁ stutaḥ ,
महायोगी महोदारः सुग्रीवेप्सितराज्यदः ॥ ११ ॥
mahā yogī maho dāraḥ sugrī vepsita rājyadaḥ .11.

____________:Today's Date

राम राम

राम राम

सुग्रीवेप्सितराज्यदः

sugrīvepsita rājyadaḥ

Glory be to Shrī Rāma, the God praised by all Divinities, the Ocean of Tranqiility, the Absolute Reality, who is worshipped by hosts of Munis, the Great Yogī, the Noble-Most, the Lord who bestowed the kingdom of Kishkindhā upon Sugrīva.

Today's Date : ________________

राम राम

सर्वपुण्याधिकफलः

sarva puṇyādhika phalaḥ

राम राम

राम राम

स्मृतसर्वाघनाशनः

smṛta
sarvāgha
nāśanaḥ

राम राम

राम राम

आदिदेवो

महादेवो

ādi devo

mahā devo

सर्वपुण्याधिकफलः स्मृतसर्वाघनाशनः ।

sarva puṇy ādhika phalaḥ smṛta sarvā ghanā śanaḥ ,

आदिदेवो महादेवो महापूरुष एव च ॥ १२ ॥

ādi devo mahā devo mahā pūruṣa eva ca .12.

_______________ :Today's Date

राम राम

राम
राम
राम
राम
राम
राम
राम
राम
राम
राम
राम
राम
राम
राम
राम
राम
राम
राम

महापुरुष एव च

राम
राम
राम
राम
राम
राम
राम
राम
राम
राम
राम
राम
राम
राम

mahā pūruṣa eva ca

राम
राम
राम
राम
राम
राम
राम
राम
राम
राम
राम
राम
राम
राम
राम
राम

Glory be to Shrī-Rāma, yield of meritorious acts, the Remover of afflictions—the Primordial Entity, the Highest God, the Supreme Being.

Today's Date : ____________________

राम राम

राम राम

पुण्योदयो दयासारः

puṇyodayo dayā sāraḥ

______________ :Today's Date

राम राम

राम
राम
राम
राम
राम
राम
राम
राम
राम
राम
राम
राम
राम
राम
राम
राम
राम
राम
राम
राम
राम
राम
राम
राम
राम
राम
राम
राम
राम
राम
राम
राम
राम
राम
राम
राम
राम
राम
राम
राम
राम
राम
राम
राम
राम
राम
राम
राम

पुराणपुरुषोत्तमः

purāṇa puruṣottamaḥ

Today's Date : ________________

राम राम

राम
राम
राम
राम
राम
राम
राम
राम
राम
राम
राम
राम
राम
राम
राम
राम
राम
राम
राम
राम
राम
राम
राम
राम
राम
राम
राम
राम
राम
राम
राम
राम
राम
राम
राम
राम
राम
राम
राम
राम
राम
राम
राम
राम
राम
राम
राम
राम
राम
राम
राम

स्मितवक्रो

मिताभाषी

smita vaktro mitā bhāṣī

पुण्योदयो दयासारः पुराणपुरुषोत्तमः ।

puṇyo dayo dayā sāraḥ purāṇa puruṣ ottamaḥ ,

स्मितवक्रो मिताभाषी पूर्वभाषी च राघवः ॥ १३ ॥

smita vaktro mitā bhāṣī pūrva bhāṣī ca rāghavaḥ .13.

_______________: *Today's Date*

पूर्वभाषी च राघवः

pūrvabhāṣī ca rāghavaḥ

Glory be to Shrī-Rāma, the source of every blessing & good furtune, the embodiment of compassion, the Supreme whose laurels are sung in the Purānas—the Lord who speaks smilingly, is reticent and mellifluent, who can speak of things to come, the brightest scion of the Raghu dynasty.

Today's Date : ____________

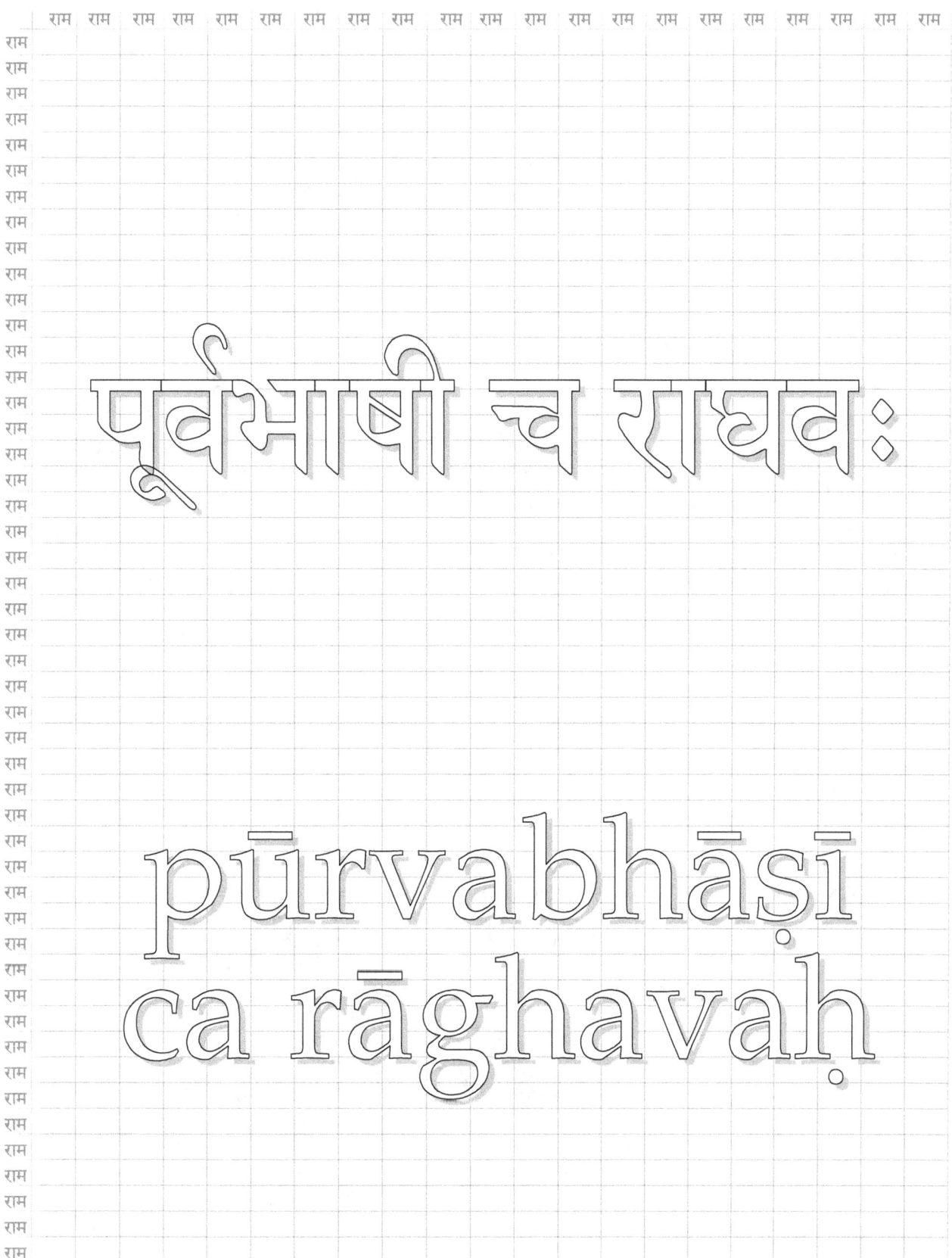

राम राम

अनन्तगुणगम्भीरो

ananta guṇa gambhīro

राम राम

______________:Today's Date

धीरोदात्तगुणोत्तमः

dhīro dātta guṇottamaḥ

राम राम

राम राम

मायामानुषचारित्रो

māyā mānuṣa cāritro

अनन्तगुणगम्भीरो धीरोदात्तगुणोत्तमः ।

ananta guṇa gambhīro dhīro dātta guṇ ottamaḥ ,

मायामानुषचारित्रो महादेवादिपूजितः ॥ १४ ॥

māyā mānuṣa cāritro mahā dev ādi pūjitaḥ .14.

_______________ :Today's Date

राम राम

राम
राम
राम
राम
राम
राम
राम
राम
राम
राम
राम
राम
राम
राम
राम
राम
राम
राम
राम
राम
राम
राम
राम
राम
राम
राम
राम
राम
राम
राम
राम
राम
राम
राम
राम
राम
राम
राम
राम
राम
राम
राम
राम
राम
राम
राम
राम
राम

महादेवादिपूजितः

mahā devādi pūjitaḥ

Glory be to Shrī-Rāma, the majestic Lord of infinite qualities, conferer of courage and superlative virtues, the God who became Incarnate presiding over Māyā—the Lord-God worshiped by God of gods Shiva & other divinities.

Today's Date : ________________

राम राम

राम
राम
राम
राम
राम
राम
राम
राम
राम
राम
राम
राम
राम
राम
राम
राम
राम
राम
राम
राम
राम
राम
राम
राम
राम
राम
राम
राम
राम
राम
राम
राम
राम
राम
राम
राम
राम
राम
राम
राम
राम
राम
राम
राम
राम
राम
राम
राम

सेतुकृज्जितवारीशः

setukṛt jitavārīśaḥ

____________:Today's Date

राम राम

राम शम राम राम राम राम राम राम

सर्वतीर्थमयो हरिः

sarva tīrthamayo hariḥ

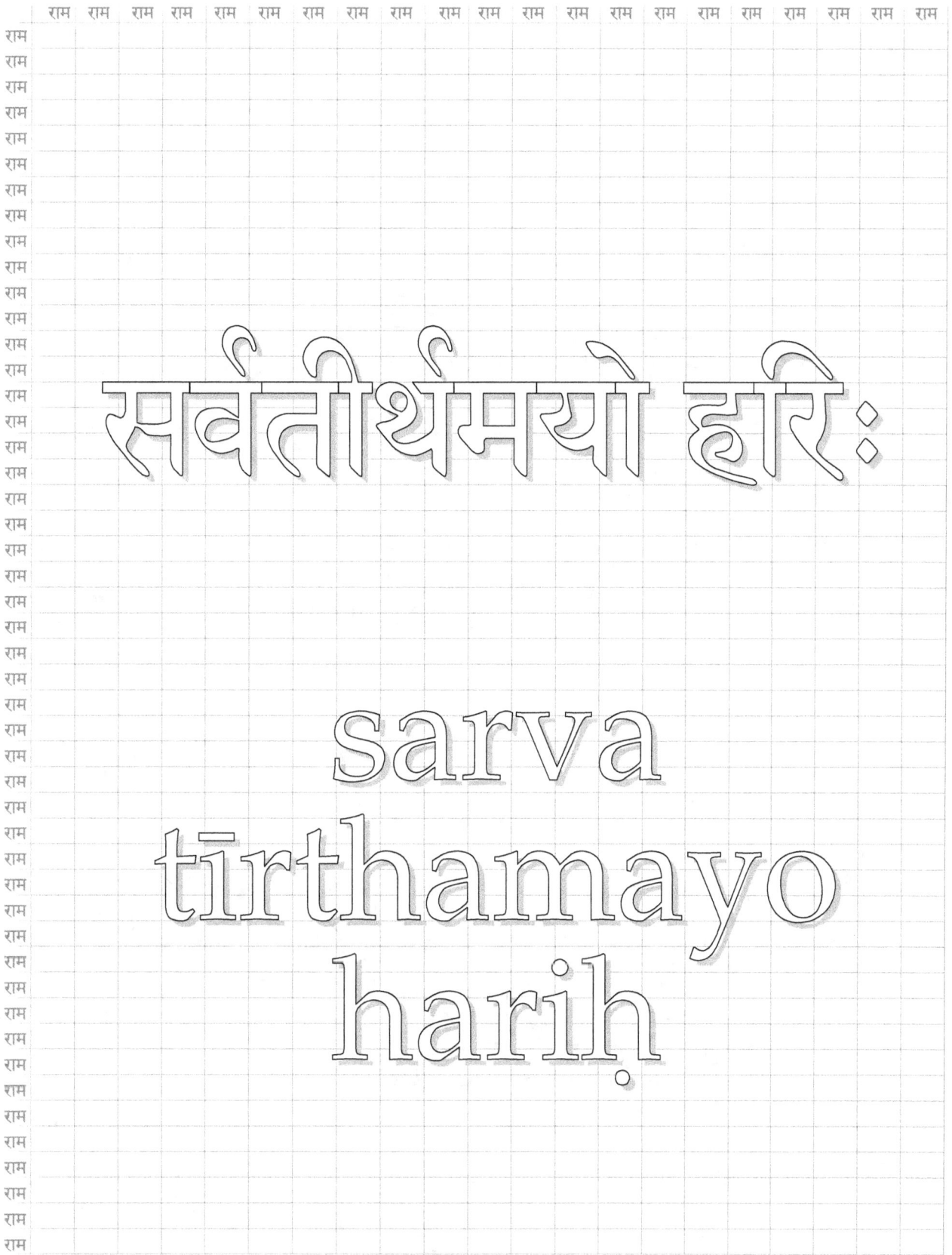

राम राम

राम राम

श्यामाङ्गः

सुन्दरः

śyām āṅgaḥ sundaraḥ

सेतुकृज्जितवारीशः सर्वतीर्थमयो हरिः ।
setu kṛ jjita vārīśaḥ sarva tīrtha mayo hariḥ ,
श्यामाङ्गः सुन्दरः शूरः पीतवासा धनुर्धरः ॥ १५ ॥
śyām āṅgaḥ sundaraḥ śūraḥ pīta vāsā dhanur dharaḥ .15.

________________ :Today's Date

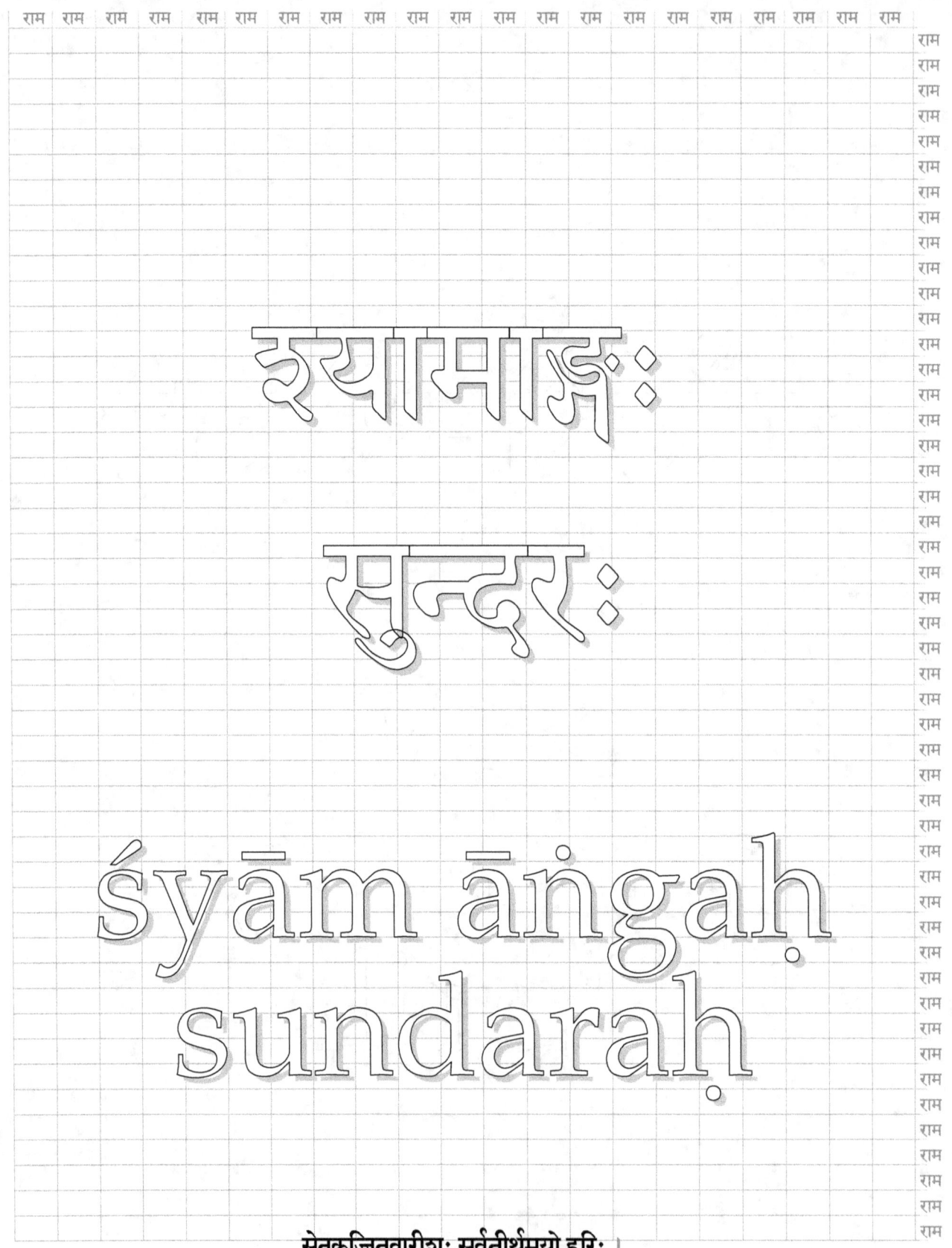

राम राम

राम राम

शूरः

पीतवासा

धनुर्धरः

śūraḥ

pīta vāsā

dhanurdharaḥ

Glory be to Shrī-Rāma who created the bridge across the ocean, the Conqueror of desires, the God who is the sum of all Holy Places, the Lord-God Uprooter of sins, the Dark-Complexioned, most Beautiful & Valiant Lord donned in yellow apparels wielding the Bow.

Today's Date : ____________________

राम राम

राम
राम
राम
राम
राम
राम
राम
राम
राम
राम
राम
राम
राम
राम
राम
राम
राम
राम
राम
राम
राम
राम
राम
राम
राम
राम
राम
राम
राम
राम
राम
राम
राम
राम
राम
राम
राम
राम
राम
राम
राम
राम
राम
राम
राम
राम
राम
राम

सर्वयज्ञाधिपो

यज्वा

sarva
yajñādhipo
yajvā

__________________:Today's Date

जरामरणवर्जितः

jarā maraṇa varjitaḥ

राम राम

राम राम

शिवलिङ्गप्रतिष्ठाता

śiva liṅga pratiṣṭhātā

सर्वयज्ञाधिपो यज्वा जरामरणवर्जितः ।

sarva yajñ ādhipo yajvā jarā maraṇa varjitaḥ ,

शिवलिङ्गप्रतिष्ठाता सर्वावगुणवर्जितः ॥ १६ ॥

śiva liṅga pratiṣṭh ātā sarvāva guṇa varjitaḥ .16.

________________:Today's Date

राम राम

राम राम

सर्वावगुणवर्जितः

sarvāvaguṇa varjitaḥ

Glory be to Shrī-Rāma, the Lord of sacrifices, the Sacrificer, He who is beyond age & death, He who installed the Shivalingam at Rāmeshwaram, the Lord bereft of evil.

Today's Date : ________________

राम राम

परमात्मा

परं ब्रह्म

paramātmā

paraṁ brahma

राम
राम
राम
राम
राम
राम
राम
राम
राम
राम
राम
राम
राम
राम
राम
राम
राम
राम
राम
राम
राम
राम
राम
राम
राम
राम
राम
राम
राम
राम
राम
राम
राम
राम
राम
राम
राम
राम
राम
राम
राम
राम
राम
राम
राम
राम
राम
राम

____________:Today's Date

सच्चिदानन्दविग्रहः

saccidānanda vigrahaḥ

Today's Date : ____________________

राम राम

राम राम

परं ज्योतिः

परंधाम

paraṁ jyotiḥ paraṁ dhāma

परमात्मा परं ब्रह्म सच्चिदानन्दविग्रहः ।

param ātmā paraṁ brahma sac cid ānanda vigrahaḥ ,

परं ज्योतिः परंधाम पराकाशः परात्परः ॥ १७ ॥

paraṁ jyotiḥ paraṁ dhāma parā kāśaḥ parā tparaḥ .17.

________________ :Today's Date

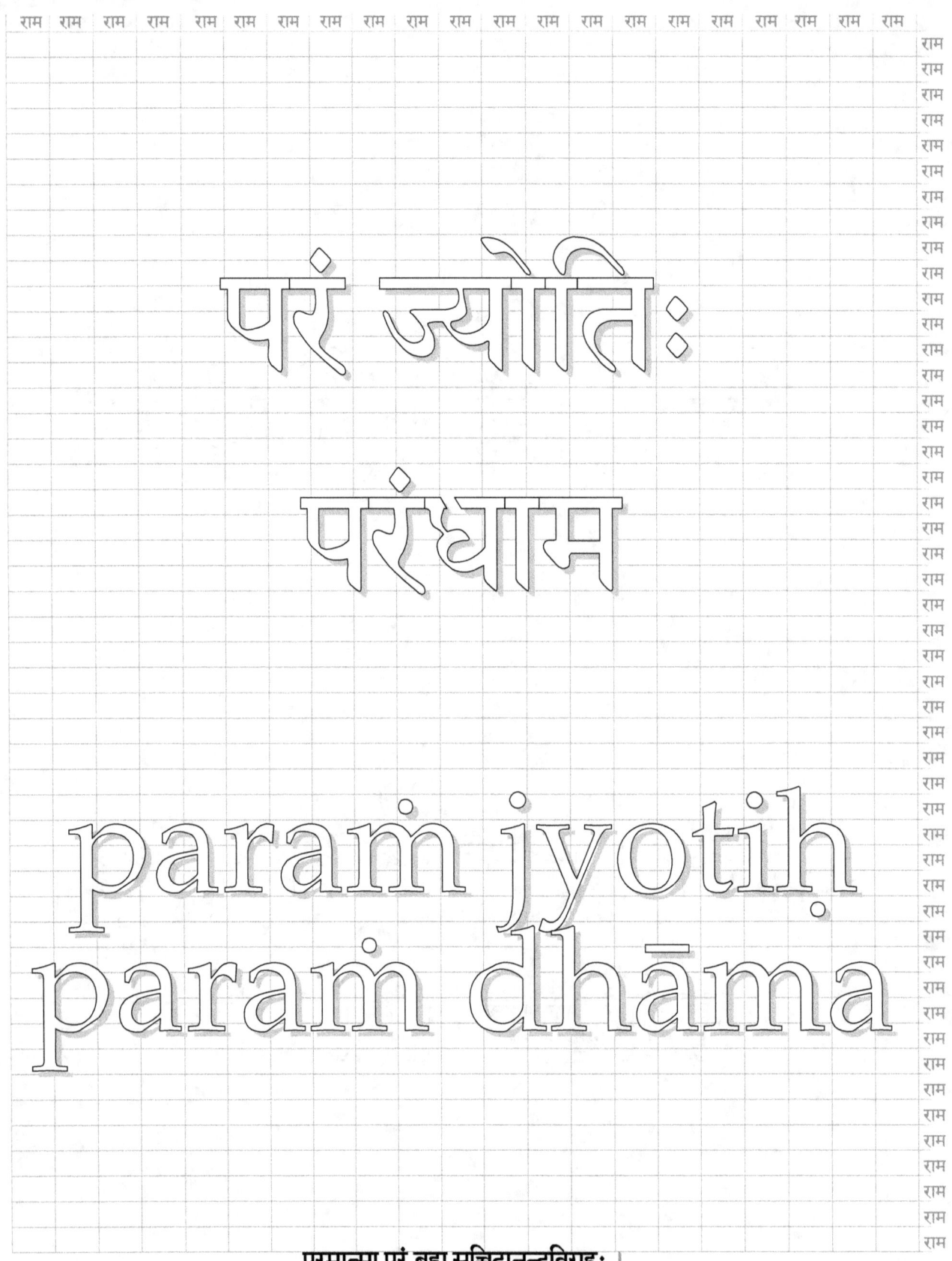

पराकाशः

परात्परः

parākāśaḥ parātparaḥ

Glory be to Shrī-Rāma, the Soul of Souls, the Supreme Absolute, the embodied Super-Consciosuness of the nature of Existence,-Knowledge-Bliss; the Fiery Light, the Final Abode, the Sovereign Space—the Highest amongst the Highest.

Today's Date : ________________

राम राम

राम
राम
राम
राम
राम
राम
राम
राम
राम
राम
राम
राम
राम
राम
राम
राम
राम
राम
राम
राम
राम
राम
राम
राम
राम
राम
राम
राम
राम
राम
राम
राम
राम
राम
राम
राम
राम
राम
राम
राम
राम
राम
राम
राम
राम
राम
राम
राम

परेशः

pareśaḥ

____________ :Today's Date

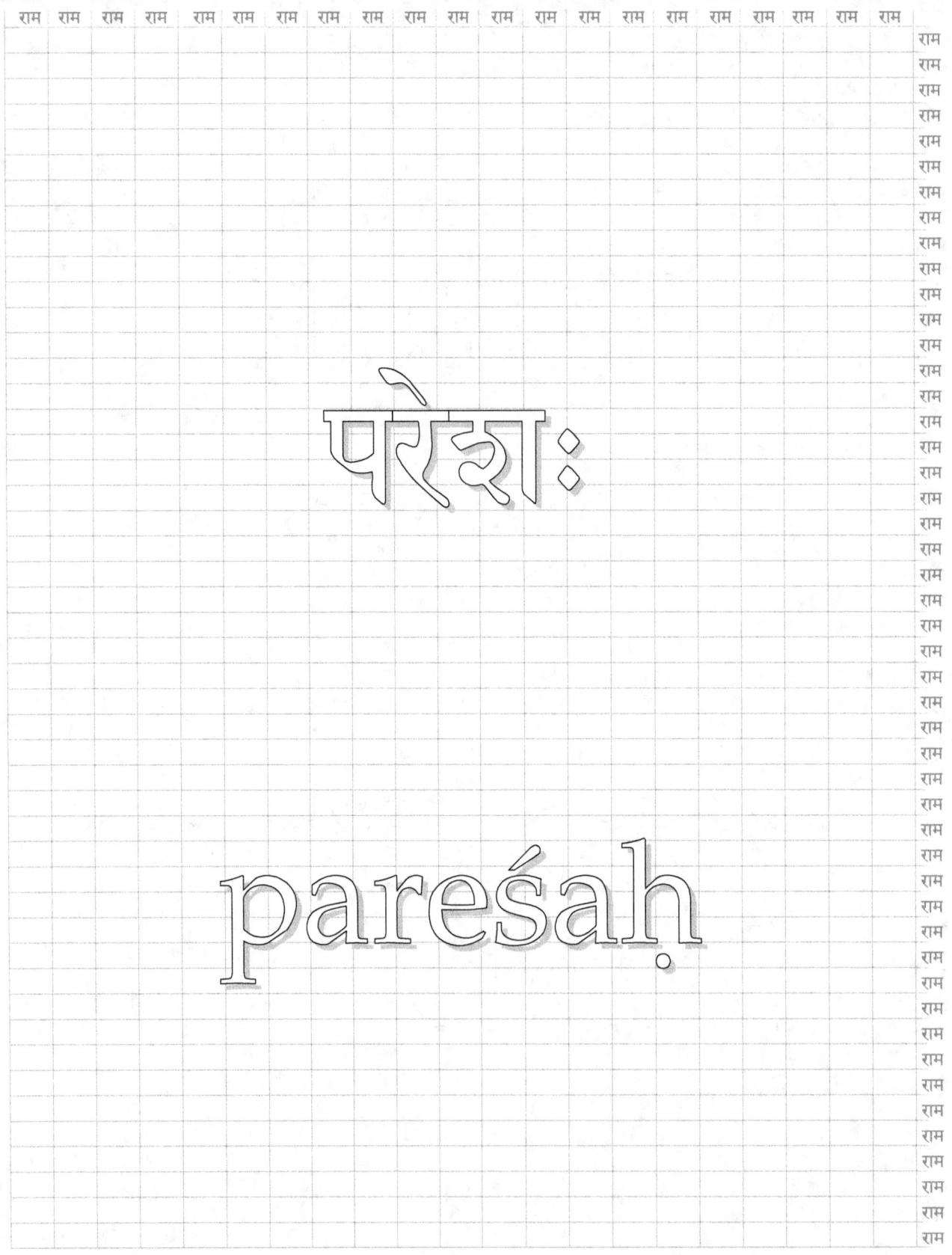

राम राम

राम राम

पारगः

pāragaḥ

राम राम

राम
राम
राम
राम
राम
राम
राम
राम
राम
राम
राम
राम
राम
राम
राम
राम
राम
राम
राम
राम
राम
राम
राम
राम
राम
राम
राम
राम
राम
राम
राम
राम
राम
राम
राम
राम
राम
राम
राम
राम
राम
राम
राम
राम
राम
राम
राम
राम

पारः

pāraḥ

परेशः पारगः पारः सर्वदेवात्मकः परः ॥

pareśaḥ pāragaḥ pāraḥ sarva devātmakaḥ paraḥ .

_________________:Today's Date

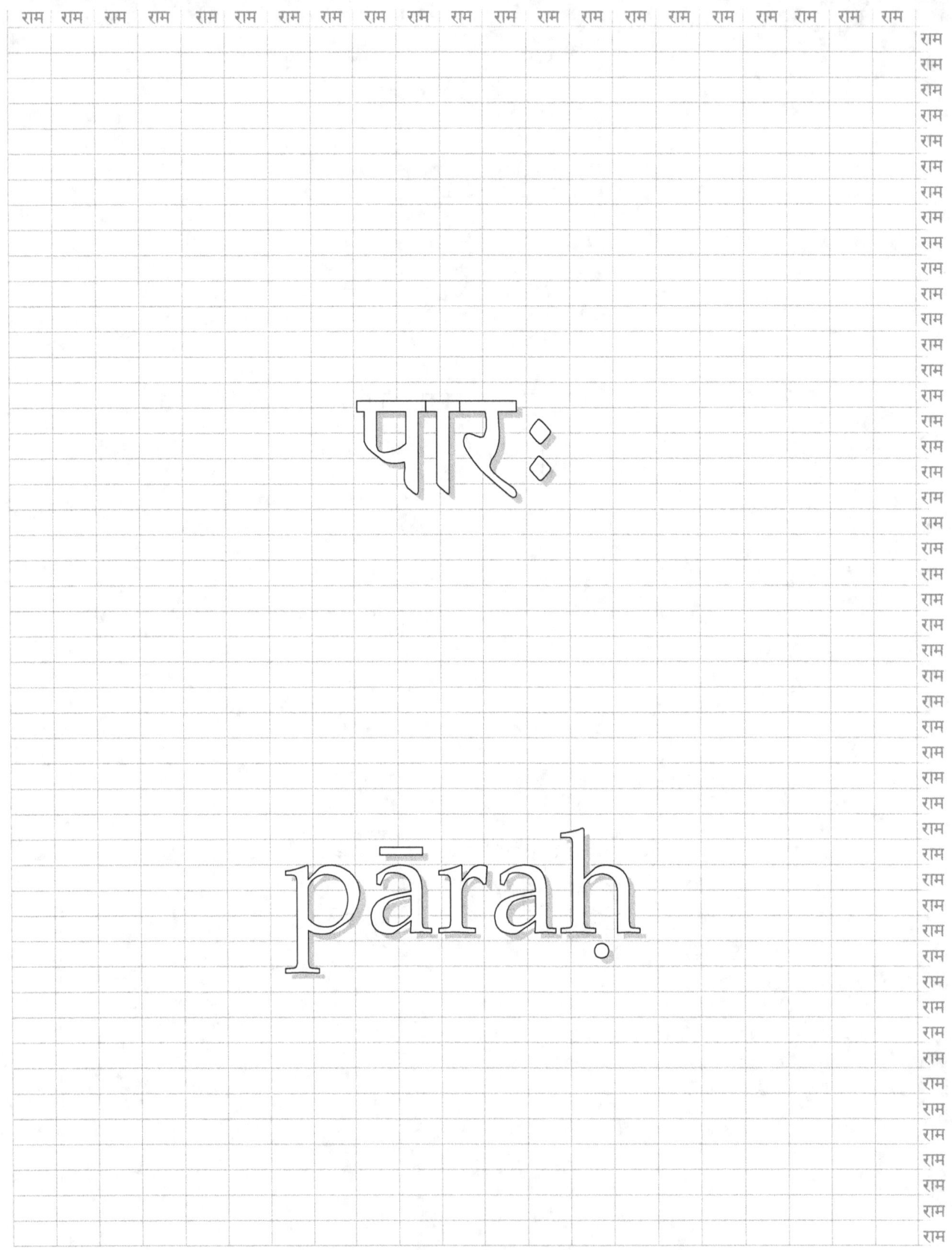

राम राम

राम राम

सर्वदेवात्मकः

परः

sarva devātmakaḥ paraḥ

Glory be to the Supreme Godhead, the Lord who takes His Devotees across the sea of births and deaths, the Transcendent Being, the Self of all gods: our Sovereign Lord-God Shrī-Rāma.

Today's Date : ________________

राम राम

इति श्रीरामाष्टोत्तर
शतनामस्तोत्रं
सम्पूर्णम्

राम
राम
राम
राम
राम
राम
राम
राम
राम
राम
राम
राम
राम
राम
राम
राम
राम
राम
राम
राम
राम
राम
राम
राम
राम
राम
राम
राम
राम
राम
राम
राम
राम
राम
राम
राम
राम
राम
राम
राम
राम
राम
राम
राम
राम
राम
राम
राम

॥ इति श्रीरामाष्टोत्तरशतनामस्तोत्रं सम्पूर्णम् ॥

. iti śrīrāmāṣṭottaraśatanāmastotraṁ sampūrṇam .

______________ :Today's Date

राम राम

राम
राम
राम
राम
राम
राम
राम
राम
राम
राम
राम
राम
राम
राम
राम
राम
राम
राम
राम
राम
राम
राम
राम
राम
राम
राम
राम
राम
राम
राम
राम
राम
राम
राम
राम
राम
राम
राम
राम
राम
राम
राम
राम
राम
राम
राम
राम
राम

iti
śrīrām
āṣṭottara
śatanāma
stotraṁ
sampūrṇam

— Thus concludes Śrī-Rāmāṣṭottara-Śatanāma-Stotraṁ - the 108 names of the Lord —

राम राम

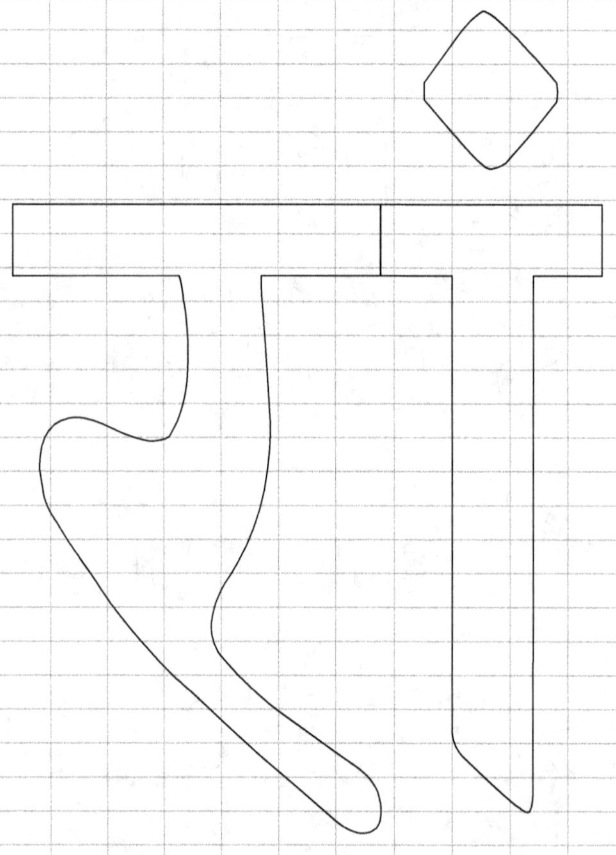

राम
राम
राम
राम
राम
राम
राम
राम
राम
राम
राम
राम
राम
राम
राम
राम
राम
राम
राम
राम
राम
राम
राम
राम
राम
राम
राम
राम
राम
राम
राम
राम
राम
राम
राम
राम
राम
राम
राम
राम
राम
राम
राम
राम
राम
राम
राम
राम

____________:Today's Date

राम राम

राम
राम
राम
राम
राम
राम
राम
राम
राम
राम
राम
राम
राम
राम
राम
राम
राम
राम
राम
राम
राम
राम
राम
राम
राम
राम
राम
राम
राम
राम
राम
राम
राम
राम
राम
राम
राम
राम
राम
राम
राम
राम
राम
राम
राम
राम
राम
राम

Today's Date : ____________

राम राम

राम
राम
राम
राम
राम
राम
राम
राम
राम
राम
राम
राम
राम
राम
राम
राम
राम
राम
राम
राम
राम
राम
राम
राम
राम
राम
राम
राम
राम
राम
राम
राम
राम
राम
राम
राम
राम
राम
राम
राम
राम
राम
राम
राम
राम
राम
राम
राम

रां राम

________________ :Today's Date

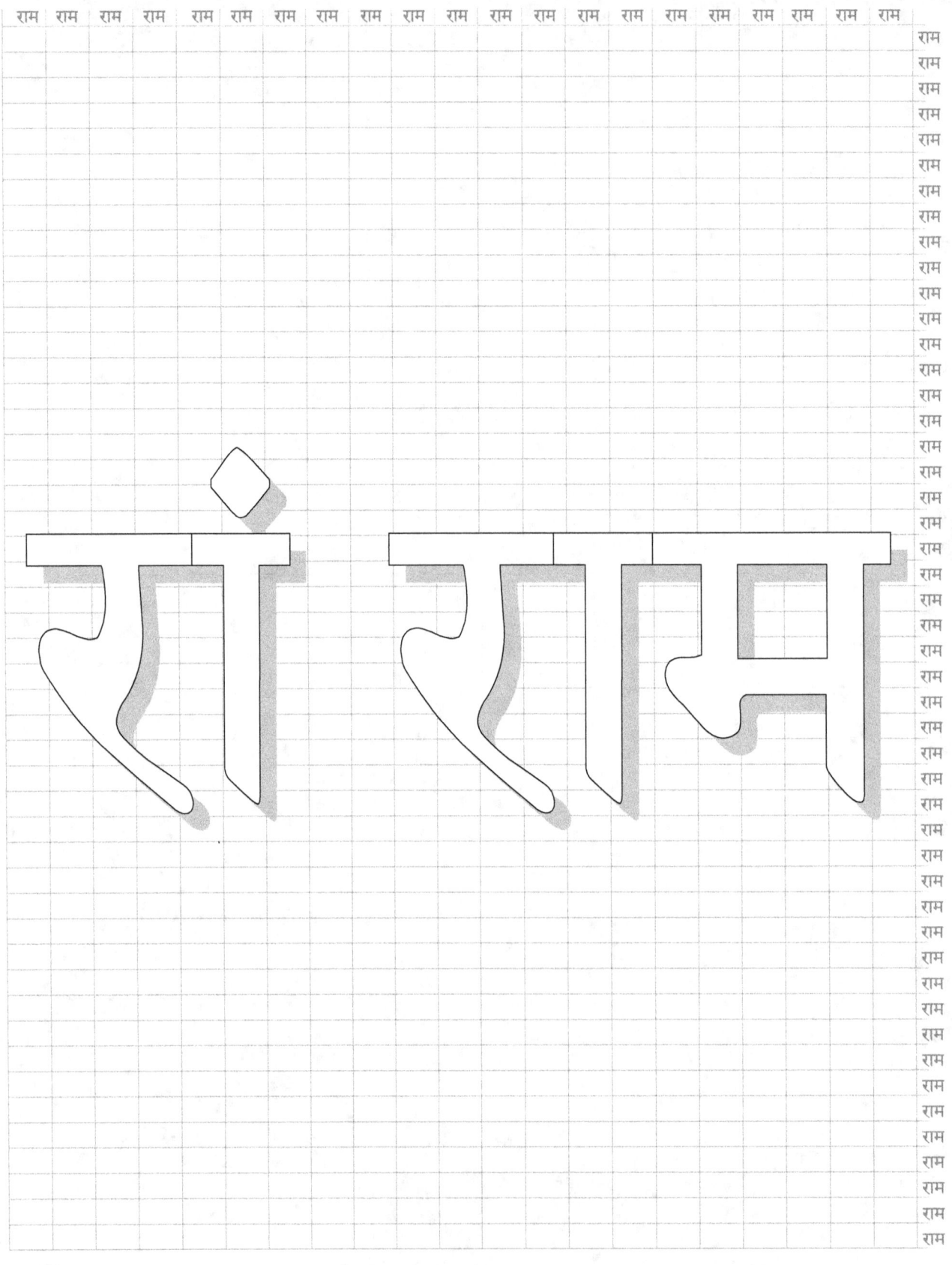

राम राम

राम
राम
राम
राम
राम
राम
राम
राम
राम
राम
राम
राम
राम
राम
राम
राम
राम
राम
राम
राम

रामचंद्र

राम
राम
राम
राम
राम
राम
राम
राम
राम
राम
राम
राम
राम
राम
राम
राम
राम
राम
राम
राम
राम
राम
राम
राम
राम
राम
राम
राम

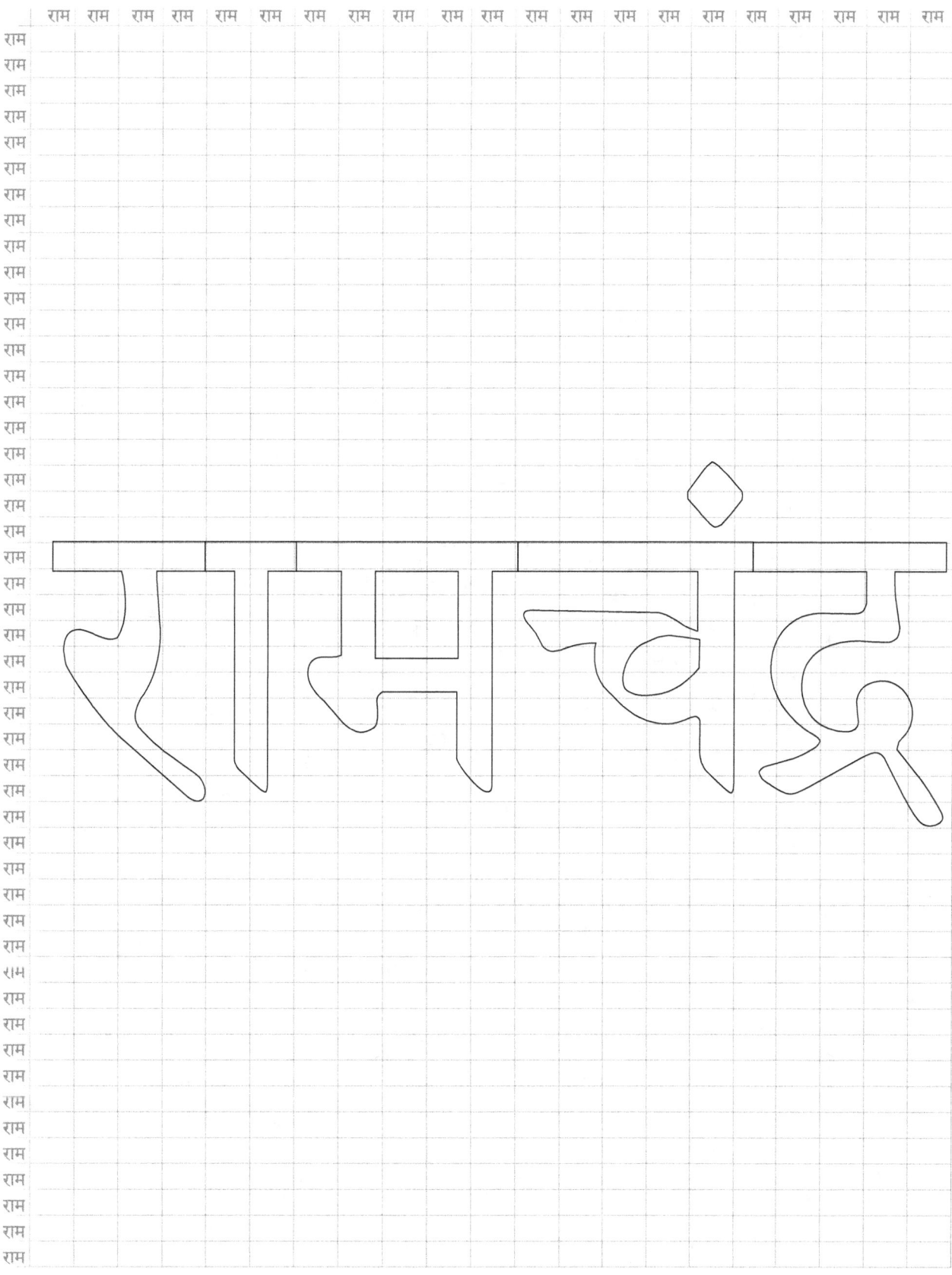

राम राम

रामभद्र

राम
राम
राम
राम
राम
राम
राम
राम
राम
राम
राम
राम
राम
राम
राम
राम
राम
राम
राम
राम
राम
राम
राम
राम
राम
राम
राम
राम
राम
राम
राम
राम
राम
राम
राम
राम
राम
राम
राम
राम
राम
राम
राम
राम
राम
राम
राम
राम

______________:Today's Date

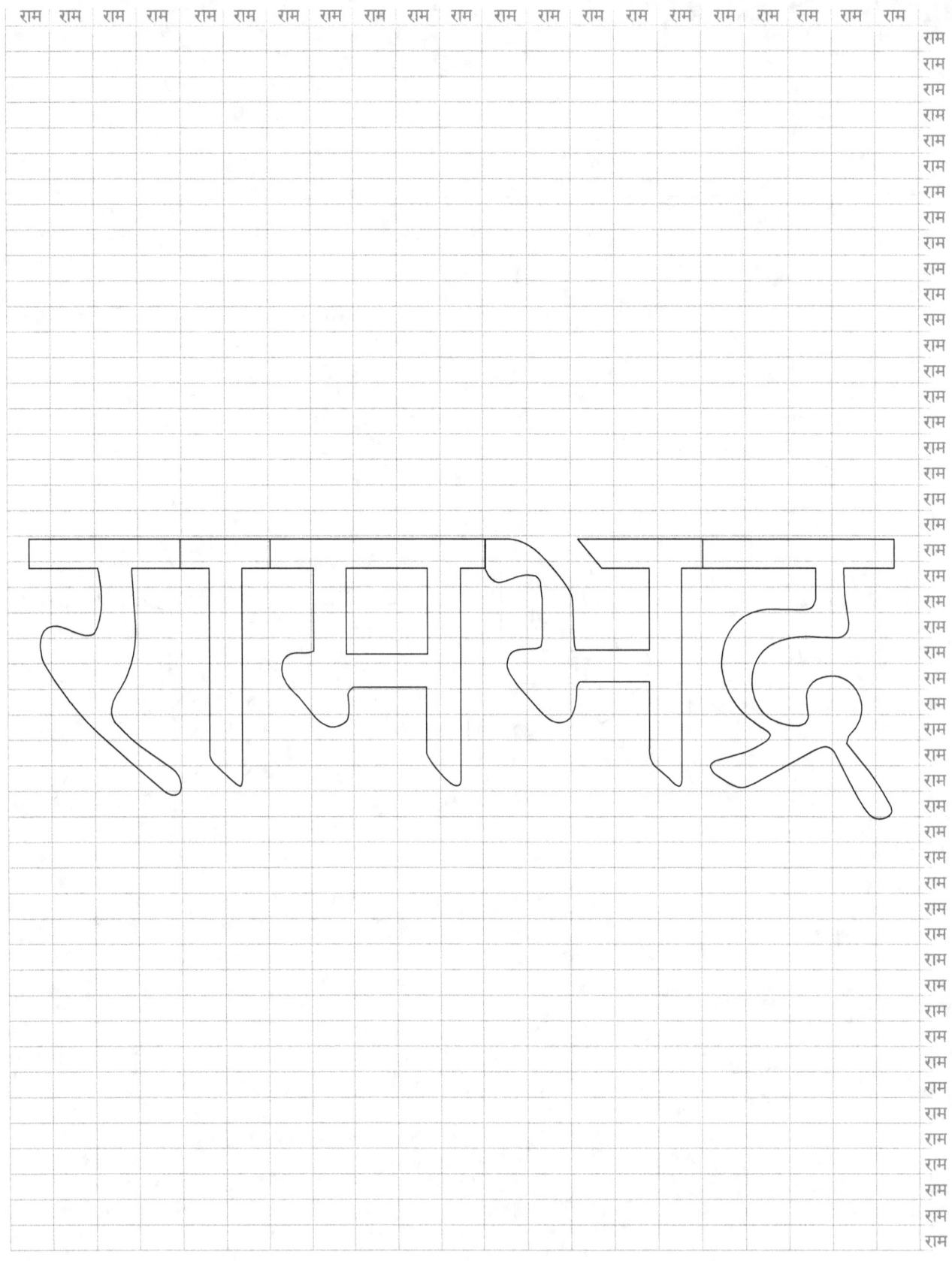

राम राम

राम
राम
राम
राम
राम
राम
राम
राम
राम
राम
राम
राम
राम
राम
राम
राम
राम
राम
राम
राम
राम
राम
राम
राम
राम
राम
राम
राम
राम
राम
राम
राम
राम
राम
राम
राम
राम
राम
राम
राम
राम
राम
राम
राम
राम
राम
राम
राम

रां

रामाय

नमः

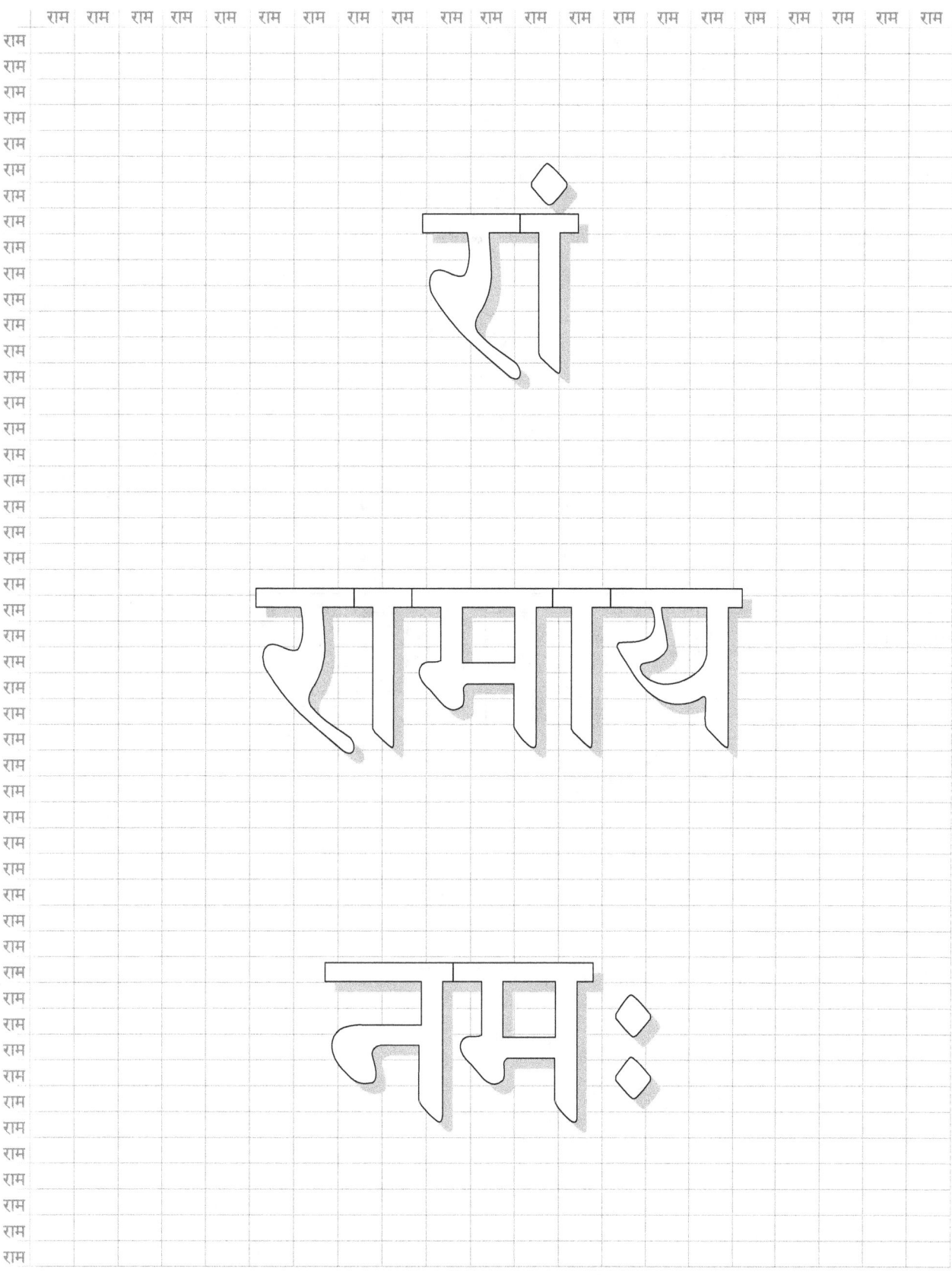

राम राम

राम
राम
राम
राम
राम
राम
राम
राम
राम
राम
राम
राम
राम
राम
राम
राम
राम
राम
राम
राम
राम
राम
राम
राम
राम
राम
राम
राम
राम
राम
राम
राम
राम
राम
राम
राम
राम
राम
राम
राम
राम
राम
राम
राम
राम
राम
राम
राम

रां

रामाय

नमः

_______________:Today's Date

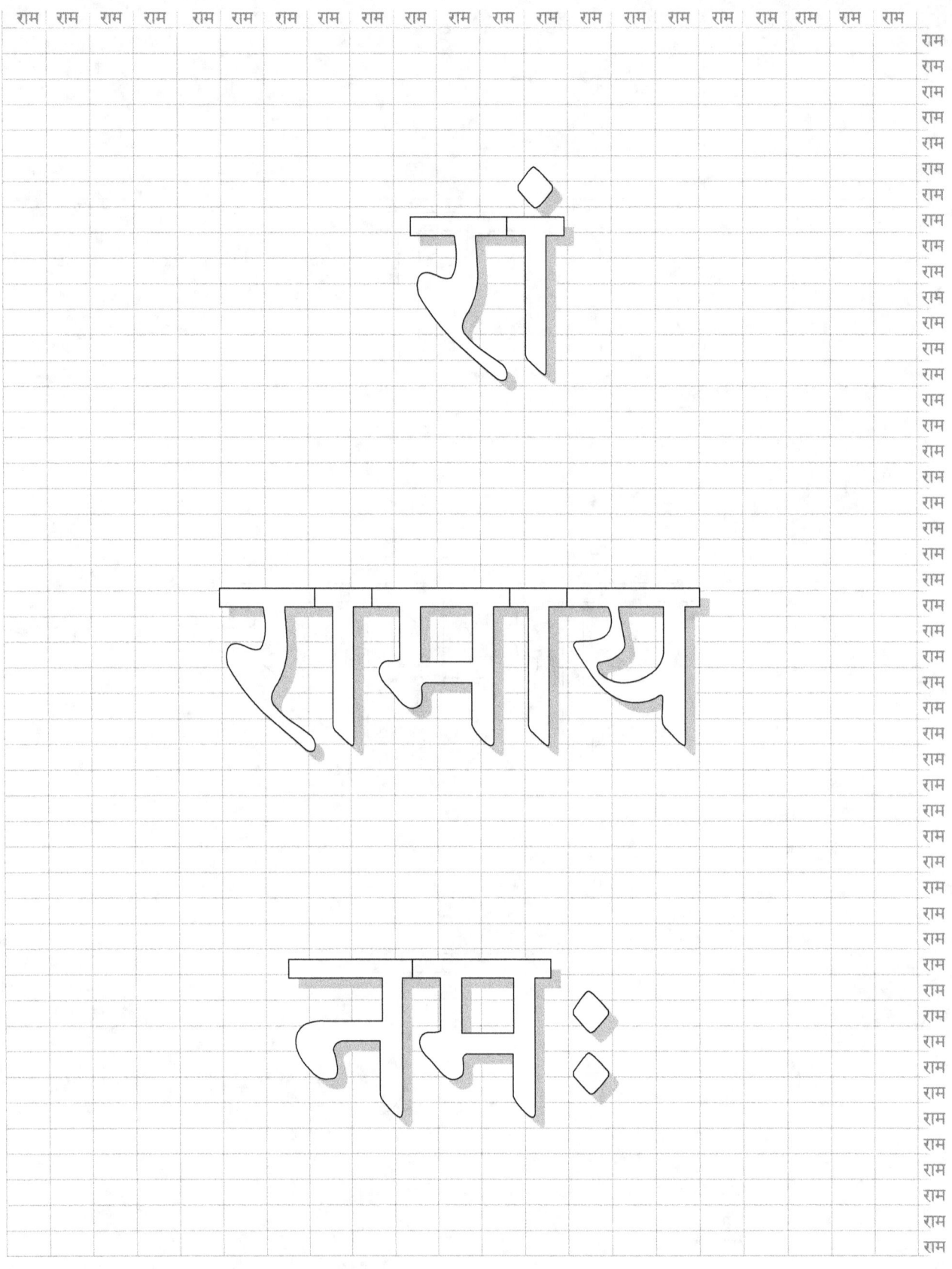

श्रीरामाष्टोत्तरशतनामस्तोत्रं

śrī-rām-āṣṭottara-śata-nāma-stotraṁ

सीताराम सीताराम सीताराम सीताराम सीताराम सीताराम

—— **The 108 Auspicious Names of Shri Rāma** ——

श्रीराघवं दशरथात्मजमप्रमेयं
śrī-rāghavaṁ daśarath-ātmajam-aprameyaṁ
सीतापतिं रघुकुलान्वयरत्नदीपम् ।
sītā-patiṁ raghu-kul-ānvaya-ratna-dīpam ,
आजानुबाहुमरविन्ददलायताक्षं
ājānu-bāhum-aravinda-dalāya-tākṣaṁ
रामं निशाचरविनाशकरं नमामि ॥
rāmaṁ niśācara-vināśa-karaṁ namāmi .

Bow I to Shrī-Rāma—son of Dasaratha, incomparable, the beloved consort of Sītā, the shining gem and leading light of the clan of Raghus—with long arms reaching upto His knees and eyes resembling petals of a lotus flower; unto Him Rāma, who is the annihilator of the night-wandering Rākshasas of the world, I offer salutations.

⌘

वैदेहीसहितं सुरद्रुमतले हैमे महामण्डपे
vaidehī-sahitaṁ sura-druma-tale haime mahā-maṇḍape
मध्ये पुष्पकमासने मणिमये वीरासने सुस्थितम् ।
madhye puṣpakam-āsane maṇi-maye vīr-āsane su-sthitam ,
अग्रे वाचयति प्रभञ्जनसुते तत्त्वं मुनिभ्यः परं
agre vāca-yati pra-bhañjana-sute tattvaṁ muni-bhyaḥ paraṁ
व्याख्यान्तं भरतादिभिः परिवृतं रामं भजे श्यामलम् ॥
vyākhy-āntaṁ bharat-ādibhiḥ pari-vṛtaṁ rāmaṁ bhaje śyāmalam .

I bow to Lord Rāma who—along with His beloved consort Sītā, daughter of Videha—is seated under the shade of Kalpavriksha (the Divine Wish-Tree) nestled in a grand gilded altar, set within the middle of the aerial Pushpaka Vimāna—upon a splendid throne constellated with gems. Encircled by brothers Bharatha and others, Rāma sits—well settled, sporting the posture of the bravest hero—while in front abides the son of Prabhanjana (Hanumān) standing in veneration, enunciating the grand maxim: that Rāma is the Supreme Truth sung of and extolled by sages.

⌘

श्रीरामो रामभद्रश्च रामचन्द्रश्च शाश्वतः ।
śrīrāmo rāma-bhadra-śca rāma-candra-śca śāśvataḥ ,
राजीवलोचनः श्रीमान् राजेन्द्रो रघुपुङ्गवः ॥ १ ॥
rājīva-locanaḥ śrīmān rājendro raghu-puṅgavaḥ .1.

Glory be to Shrī Rāma, Bestower of Felicity, the all-auspicious Lord, shining like the full-moon, the eternal Divine-Being of lotus-eyes, abode of Laxmi, King-of-Kings, the grandest Scion of the Dynasty of Raghus.

⌘

जानकीवल्लभो जैत्रो जितामित्रो जनार्दनः ।
jānakī-vallabho jaitro jitā-mitro jan-ārdanaḥ ,
विश्वामित्रप्रियो दान्तः शरणत्राणतत्परायः ॥ २ ॥
viśvā-mitra-priyo dāntaḥ śaraṇa-trāṇa-tatparāyḥ .2.

Glory be to the Beloved of Jānakī, the ever-victorious, vanquisher of foes, the redeemer of beings, dearest disciple of Vishwāmitra, self-disciplined, ever determined to protect those who take refuge in Him.

⌘

वालिप्रमथनो वाग्मी सत्यवाक् सत्यविक्रमः ।
vāli-pra-mathano vāgmī satyavāk satya-vikramaḥ ,
सत्यव्रतो व्रतधरः सदा हनुमदाश्रितः ॥ ३ ॥
satya-vrato vrata-dharaḥ sadā hanumad-āśritaḥ .3.

Glory be to the Victor of Vāli, the Eloquent One, of Truthful speech, valiant in defending the Truth—of truthful Vows, practician of penance, the Lord-God ever served under the aegis of Shrī Hanumān.

⌘

कौसलेयः खरध्वंसी विराधवधपण्डितः ।
kausal-eyaḥ khara-dhvaṁsī virādha-vadha-paṇḍitaḥ ,
विभीषणपरित्राता हरकोदण्डखण्डनः ॥ ४ ॥
vibhīṣaṇa-pari-trātā hara-kodaṇḍa-khaṇḍanaḥ .4.

Glory be to Kausalyā's son, Destroyer of the demon Khara, skillful in subjugating the monster Virādha, the Protector of Vibhishan—the One who broke the mighty Bow of Shiva.

⌘

सप्ततालप्रभेत्ता च दशग्रीवशिरोहरः ।
sapta-tāla-pra-bhettā ca daśa-grīva-śiro-haraḥ ,
जामदग्न्यमहादर्पदलनस्ताटकान्तकः ॥ ५ ॥
jāma-dagnya-mahā-darpa-dalanas-tāṭak-āntakaḥ .5.

Glory be to the Valorous Rāma who pierced the seven Tāla Trees with a single arrow, who cut off the ten-heads of Rāvan, who shattered the inordinate arrogance of Jamadagni's son, and who slew Tāṭakā the terrible demon.

⌘

वेदान्तसारो वेदात्मा भवरोगस्य भेषजम् ।
vedānta-sāro ved-ātmā bhava-rogasya bheṣajam ,
दूषणत्रिशिरो हन्ता त्रिमूर्तिस्त्रिगुणात्मकः ॥ ६ ॥
dūṣaṇa-tri-śiro hantā tri-mūrtis-trigun-ātmakaḥ .6.

Glory be to Rāma, the Essence of Vedānta, the Personification of the Vedas, Reliever of all earthly ailments, the slayer of monsters Dūṣaṇa & Triśira, the Lord-God manifest as the Trinity of Brahmmā, Vishnu, Mahesh—and from whom emanate the three gunas of Māyā.

त्रिविक्रमस्त्रिलोकात्मा पुण्यचारित्रकीर्तनः ।
tri-vikramas-trilok-ātmā puṇya-cāritra-kīrtanaḥ ,
त्रिलोकरक्षको धन्वी दण्डकारण्यपावनः ॥ ७ ॥
tri-loka-rakṣako dhanvī daṇḍak-āraṇya-pāvanaḥ .7.

Glory be to the Lord who spanned the Three-Regions of the Universe with His feet, the Lord-God pervaded throughout earth, hell and heaven, whose hallowed deeds are sung through Hymns, who's the Protector of the Three-Worlds, the Wielder of the Bow, and who sanctifed the Dandaka forest by dwelling there.

⌘

अहल्याशापशमनः पितृभक्तो वरप्रदः ।
ahalyā-śāpa-śamanaḥ pitṛ-bhakto vara-pradaḥ ,
जितेन्द्रियो जितक्रोधो जितामित्रो जगद्गुरुः ॥ ८ ॥
jit-endriyo jita-krodho jitā-mitro jagad-guruḥ .8.

Glory be to Shrī-Rāma, the Remover of Ahalyā's curse, ever devoted to His father Dashrath, the Conferrer of boons, Conqueror of sense-organs, the Victor over anger, who wins over friends—and who is the supreme Guru of the whole world.

⌘

ऋक्षवानरसंघाती चित्रकूटसमाश्रयः ।
ṛkṣa-vānara-saṁghātī citra-kūṭa-sam-āśrayaḥ ,
जयन्तत्राणवरदः सुमित्रापुत्रसेवितः ॥ ९ ॥
jayanta-trāṇa-varadaḥ sumitrā-putra-sevitaḥ .9.

Glory be to Shrī-Rāma—the Lord who presided over the hosts of bears and monkeys, who dwelt at the Chitrakūta Hill, who saved Jayanta—the Lord-God ever served by Sumitrā's son Lakshman.

⌘

सर्वदेवादिदेवश्च मृतवानरजीवनः ।
sarva-dev-ādi-deva-śca mṛta-vānara-jīvanaḥ ,
मायामारीचहन्ता च महादेवो महाभुजः ॥ १० ॥
māyā-mārīca-hantā ca mahā-devo mahā-bhujaḥ .10.

Glory be to the God of gods Rāma—the Lord who revived the dead monkeys, the slayer of Maricha, the illusion practicing demon—the Greatest-God of mighty arms.

⌘

सर्वदेवस्तुतः सौम्यो ब्रह्मण्यो मुनिसंस्तुतः ।
sarva-deva-stutaḥ saumyo brahm-aṇyo muni-saṁ-stutaḥ ,
महायोगी महोदारः सुग्रीवेप्सितराज्यदः ॥ ११ ॥
mahā-yogī maho-dāraḥ sugrī-vepsita-rājyadaḥ .11.

Glory be to Shrī Rāma, the God praised by all Divinities, the Ocean of Tranqiility, the Absolute Reality, who is worshipped by hosts of Munis, the Great Yogī, the Noble-Most, the Lord who bestowed the kingdom of Kishkindhā upon Sugrīva.

⌘

सर्वपुण्याधिकफलः स्मृतसर्वाघनाशनः ।
sarva-puṇy-ādhika-phalaḥ smṛta-sarvā-ghanā-śanaḥ ,
आदिदेवो महादेवो महापूरुष एव च ॥ १२ ॥
ādi-devo mahā-devo mahā-pūruṣa eva ca .12.

Glory be to Shrī-Rāma, yield of meritorious acts, the Remover of afflictions—the Primordial Entity, the Highest God, the Supreme Being.

⌘

पुण्योदयो दयासारः पुराणपुरुषोत्तमः ।
puṇyo-dayo dayā-sāraḥ purāṇa-puruṣ-ottamaḥ ,
स्मितवक्त्रो मिताभाषी पूर्वभाषी च राघवः ॥ १३ ॥
smita-vaktro mitā-bhāṣī pūrva-bhāṣī ca rāghavaḥ .13.

Glory be to Shrī-Rāma, the source of every blessing & good furtune, the embodiment of compassion, the Supreme whose laurels are sung in the Purānas—the Lord who speaks smilingly, is reticent and mellifluent, who can speak of things to come, the brightest scion of the Raghu dynasty.

⌘

अनन्तगुणगम्भीरो धीरोदात्तगुणोत्तमः ।
ananta-guṇa-gambhīro dhīro-dātta-guṇ-ottamaḥ ,
मायामानुषचारित्रो महादेवादिपूजितः ॥ १४ ॥
māyā-mānuṣa-cāritro mahā-dev-ādi-pūjitaḥ .14.

Glory be to Shrī-Rāma, the majestic Lord of infinite qualities, conferer of courage and superlative virtues, the God who became Incarnate presiding over Māyā—the Lord-God worshiped by God of gods Shiva & other divinities.

⌘

सेतुकृज्जितवारीशः सर्वतीर्थमयो हरिः ।
setu-kṛ-jjita-vārīśaḥ sarva-tīrtha-mayo hariḥ ,
श्यामाङ्गः सुन्दरः शूरः पीतवासा धनुर्धरः ॥ १५ ॥
śyām-āṅgaḥ sundaraḥ śūraḥ pīta-vāsā dhanur-dharaḥ .15.

Glory be to Shrī-Rāma who created the bridge across the ocean, the Conqueror of desires, the God who is the sum of all Holy Places, the Lord-God Uprooter of sins, the Dark-Complexioned, most Beautiful & Valiant Lord donned in yellow apparels wielding the Bow.

⌘

सर्वयज्ञाधिपो यज्वा जरामरणवर्जितः ।
sarva-yajñ-ādhipo yajvā jarā-maraṇa-varjitaḥ ,
शिवलिङ्गप्रतिष्ठाता सर्वावगुणवर्जितः ॥ १६ ॥
śiva-liṅga-pratiṣṭh-ātā sarvāva-guṇa-varjitaḥ .16.

Glory be to Shrī-Rāma, the Lord of sacrifices, the Sacrificer, He who is beyond age & death, He who installed the Shivalingam at Rāmeshwaram, the Lord bereft of evil.

⌘

परमात्मा परं ब्रह्म सच्चिदानन्दविग्रहः ।

param-ātmā paraṁ brahma sac-cid-ānanda-vigrahaḥ ,

परं ज्योतिः परंधाम पराकाशः परात्परः ॥ १७ ॥

paraṁ jyotiḥ paraṁ-dhāma parā-kāśaḥ parā-tparaḥ .17.

Glory be to Shrī-Rāma, the Soul of Souls, the Supreme Absolute, the embodied Super-Consciosuness of the nature of Existence,-Knowledge-Bliss; the Fiery Light, the Final Abode, the Sovereign Space—the Highest amongst the Highest.

⌘

परेशः पारगः पारः सर्वदेवात्मकः परः ॥

pareśaḥ pāragaḥ pāraḥ sarva-devātmakaḥ paraḥ .

Glory be to the Supreme Godhead, the Lord who takes His Devotees across the sea of births and deaths, the Transcendent Being, the Self of all gods: our Sovereign Lord-God Shrī-Rāma.

⌘

॥ इति श्रीरामाष्टोत्तरशतनामस्तोत्रं सम्पूर्णम् ॥

. iti śrīrāmāṣṭottaraśatanāmastotraṁ sampūrṇam .

— Thus ends Śrī-Rāmāṣṭottara-Śatanāma-Stotraṁ - the 108 names of the Lord —

(Author of this Original Sanskrit Hymn is: Shrī Vyāsa-Deva [Pre-historic Sage]. Translator: Sushma)

www.ingramcontent.com/pod-product-compliance
Lightning Source LLC
Chambersburg PA
CBHW080026130526
44591CB00037B/2682
* 9 7 8 1 9 4 5 7 3 9 2 6 2 *